Praise for *Unraveled*

My advice to anyone interested in taking their understanding, and practice of, yoga to the next level is to go and get *Unraveled* today. Erin Evans uses the profound knowledge of the subject she has gained as a yoga practitioner and teacher to unlock the wisdom contained in the Patanjali sutras for the modern reader.
Trissa Tismal-Capili | USA Today and Wall Street Journal Bestselling Author, and Entrepreneur Flow Expert

The invaluable knowledge contained in the yoga sutras has never been more accessible than in the pages of *Unraveled*. Yoga expert Erin Evans understands that the practice of yoga is as much about spiritual enlightenment—being present—as it is about physical flexibility. In the book's pages, she masterfully brings the ancient wisdom of the sutras to life with modern examples that prove their relevance in today's world.
Tamara Nall | CEO & Founder, The Leading Niche

If practicing yoga seems to you like a spiritual, as well as physical, experience, read *Unraveled* to learn why your intuition is accurate. Yoga expert Erin Evans explains the surpassing wisdom of the yoga sutras, which make it clear that the physical postures the practice uses, when combined with these nuggets of timeless wisdom, are healthy for both body and soul. Long live Yoga!
Grace Flores-Hughes | Author/Consultant, F&H 2 Inc.

If you want to get more out of your yoga routine, run don't walk to your nearest bookstore, digital or physical, and pick up a copy of this book. *Unraveled*, by expert yogi Erin Evans, explains in practical, modern English how the ancient wisdom contained in the yoga sutras is more useful than ever today.

Michael Brainard | CEO, Brainard Strategy; Bestselling Author of *How to Become an Effective Leader*

The sages who wrote the yoga sutras understood that the impact of the practice's poses, or asanas, could be magnified by a set of principles, or sutras, emphasizing behaviors that support and expand the peace of mind enabled by the exercises. Erin Evans has done a brilliant job of bringing the wisdom contained in these sutras to life by providing translations of them from Sanskrit along with examples demonstrating how readers can put them to use in their own lives.

Dr. Kathy Humel | CEO, Senior Consultant RxKHumel, LLC; Bestselling Author of *Sweetie, That's Not Sweets!*

UNRAVELED

A Modern Look at the Yoga Sutras

ERIN EVANS

Copyright © 2023 **Erin Evans**
Published in the United States by Leaders Press.
www.leaderspress.com

All rights reserved. No part of this book may be reproduced or transmitted in any form or by any means, electronic or mechanical, including photocopying, recording, or by an information storage and retrieval system – except by a reviewer who may quote brief passages in a review to be printed in a magazine or newspaper – without permission in writing from the publisher.

ISBN 978-1-63735-188-8 (pbk)
ISBN 978-1-63735-189-5 (ebook)

Library of Congress Control Number: **2023901190**

To my family, Calvin, Debra, Allison, and Micah, for supporting and instigating my wild dreams.

To my friends, teachers, and students—without you, none of this matters.

Contents

Preface xv

The Teacher-Student Prayer xviii

The Ashtanga Opening Invocation xix

1 *Samādhi Pāda Sutras* 1

1.1. The Practice of Yoga Starts Now! 2

1.2. When the Fluctuations of the Mind Stop, Yoga Happens 3

1.3. Then the Seer Dwells in Their Own True Splendor 4

1.4. At Other Times, the Seer Identifies with the
Fluctuations of the Mind 5

1.5. The Movements of Consciousness Are Fivefold. They Are
Cognizable or Noncognizable, Painful or Not Painful 6

1.6. They Are Caused by Correct Knowledge, Illusion,
Delusion, Sleep, and Memory 8

1.7. Correct Knowledge Is Direct, Inferred, or Proven as Factual 9

1.8. Erroneous Knowledge Is Based on the Nonfact, or the Nonreal 9

1.9. Verbal Knowledge Void of Substance Is Imagination 10

1.10. Sleep Is the Nondeliberate Absence of Thought
Waves and Knowledge 10

1.11. Memory Is the Unmodified Recollection of
Words and Experiences 11

1.12. Commit to Your Practice without Attachments in
Order to Still the Mind 12

1.13. Practice Is the Steadfast Effort to Still These Fluctuations 13

1.14. Long, Uninterrupted, Alert Practice Is the Firm Foundation for Restraining the Fluctuations 14

1.15. Renunciation Is the Practice of Detachment from Desires. 16

1.16. When One Gains Knowledge of Spirit (*Puruṣa*), They Cease to Thirst for the Manifestations of the World (*the Gunas*) 16

1.17. Practice and Detachment Develop Four Types of *Samādhi*: Self-Analysis, Synthesis, Bliss, and Experience of Pure Being 18

1.18. The Void Arising in These Experiences Is Another *Samādhi*. Hidden Impressions Lie Dormant but Spring Up during Moments of Awareness, Creating Fluctuations to the Purity of Consciousness 19

1.19. In This State, One May Experience Bodylessness or Become Merged in Nature. This May Lead to Isolation or to a State of Loneliness 21

1.20. Practice Must Be Pursued with Trust, Confidence, Vigor, Keen Memory, and Power of Absorption to Break Spiritual Complacency 21

1.21. The Goal Is Near for Those Who Are Supremely Vigorous and Intense in Practice 24

1.22. There Is a Difference between Those Who Are Mild, Average, and Keen in Their Practices 25

1.23. The Mind May Be Restrained by Profound Meditation and Surrender to God 26

1.24. God Is Untouched by Conflicts, Actions, and Cause and Effect 27

1.25. God Is the Unexcelled Seed of All Knowledge 28

1.26. God Is the First, Foremost, and Absolute Guru, Unconditioned by Time 29

1.27. He Is Represented by the Sacred Syllable *Aum*, Called *Pranava* 31

1.28. The Mantra *Aum* Is to Be Repeated Constantly, with Feeling, Realizing Its Full Significance 31

1.29. Meditation on God with the Repetition of *Aum* Removes Obstacle to the Mastery of the Inner Self 32

1.30. These Obstacles Are Disease, Inertia, Doubt, Heedlessness,
Laziness, Indiscipline of the Senses, Erroneous Views,
Lack of Perseverance, and Backsliding 33

1.31. Sorrow, Despair, Unsteadiness of the Body, and
Irregular Breathing Further Distract the Citta 38

1.32. Adherence to Single-Minded Effort Prevents
These Impediments 39

1.33. We Must Have Friendship for All. We Must Be
Merciful toward Those That Are in Misery. When People
Are Happy, We Ought to Be Happy, and to the Wicked,
We Must Be Indifferent 40

1.34. Or by Maintaining the Pensive State Felt at the
Time of Soft and Steady Exhalation and during Passive
Retention after Exhalation 43

1.35. Or by Contemplating an Object That Helps to
Maintain Steadiness of the Mind and Consciousness 43

1.36. Or Inner Stability Is Gained by Contemplating a
Luminous, Sorrowless, Effulgent Light 44

1.37. Or by Contemplating on Enlightened Sages Who
Are Free from Desires and Attachments or Divine Objects 45

1.38. Or by Recollecting and Contemplating the Experiences
of Dream-Filled or Dreamless Sleep during a Watchful
Waking State 46

1.39. Or by Meditating on Any Desired Object Conducive
to Steadiness of Consciousness 47

1.40. Mastery of Contemplation Brings the Power to
Extend from the Finest Particle to the Greatest Particles
to Infinity 48

1.41. The Yogi Realizes That the Knower, the Instrument of
Knowing, and the Known Are One, Himself, the Seer.
Like a Pure Transparent Jewel, He Reflects an
Unsullied Purity 50

1.42. At This Stage, Called *Savitarkā Samāpatti,* the Word,
the Meaning, and the Content Reblended, and
Become Special Knowledge 51

1.43. In *Nirvitarka Samapatti,* the Difference between Memory
and Intellectual Illumination Is Disclosed: Memory Is
Cleansed and Consciousness Shines without Reflection 52

1.44. The Contemplation of Subtle Aspects Is Similarly
Explained as Deliberate or Nondeliberate 53

1.45. The Subtlest Level of Nature (*Prakriti*) Is Consciousness.
When Consciousness Is Dissolved in Nature, It Loses All
Marks and Becomes Pure 54

1.46. The States of *Samādhi* Described in the Previous Sutras
Are Dependent upon a Support or Seed and Are
Termed *Sabīja* 54

1.47. From Proficiency in *Nirvicāra Sampatti* Comes Purity.
Sattva, or Luminosity, Flows Undisturbed, Kindling the
Spiritual Light of the Self 55

1.48. When Consciousness Dwells in Wisdom, a Truth-Bearing
State of Direct Spiritual Perception Dawns 55

1.49. This Truth-Bearing Knowledge and Wisdom Is Distinct
from and beyond the Knowledge Gleaned from Books,
Testimony, or Inference 56

1.50. A New Life Begins with This Truth-Bearing Light.
Previous Impressions Are Left Behind, and New
Ones Are Prevented 56

1.51. When the New Light of Wisdom Is Also Relinquished,
Seedless *Samādhi* Dawns 57

2 *Sādhana Pāda Sutras* 61

2.1. Burning Zeal in Practice, Self-Study, Study of Scriptures,
and Surrender to God Are the Facts of Yoga 63

2.2. The Practice of Yoga Reduces Afflictions and
Leads to *Samādhi* 64

2.3. The Five Afflictions Which Distort Consciousness
Are Ignorance, Ego, Pride, Aversion, and Fear of Death. 65

2.4. Lack of True Knowledge Is the Source of All Pains
and Sorrows whether Dormant, Interrupted, or Fully Active. 66

2.5. Mistaking the Transient for the Permanent, the Impure
for the Pure, Pain for Pleasure, and That Which Is Not
Self of the Self—This Is Called Lack of Spiritual Knowledge 67

2.6. Egoism Is the Identification of the Seer with the
Instrumental Power of Seeing 68

2.7. Pleasure Leads to Desire and Emotional Attachment 69

2.8. Unhappiness Leads to Hatred 69

2.9. Self-Preservation or Attachment to Life Is the Subtlest
of All Afflictions. It Is Found Even in Wise Men 70

2.10. Subtle Afflictions Are to Be Minimized and Eradicated
by the Process of Involution 71

2.11. The Fluctuations of Consciousness Created by Gross
and Subtle Afflictions Are to Be Silenced through
Meditation 72

2.12. The Accumulated Imprints of Past Lives, Rooted in
Afflictions, Will Be Experienced in Present and
Future Lives 73

2.13. As long as the Root of Actions Exists, It Will Give Rise
to Class of Birth, Span of Life, and Experiences 74

2.14. According to Our Good, Bad, or Mixed Actions, the
Quality of Our Life, Its Span, and the Nature of Birth Are
Experienced as Being Pleasant or Painful 76

2.15. The Wise Person Knows That Owing to the Fluctuations,
the Qualities of Nature, and Subliminal Impressions,
Even Pleasant Experience Are Tinged with Sorrow,
and He Keeps Aloof from Them 76

2.16. The Pains Which Are Yet to Come Can Be and
Are to Be Avoided 77

2.17. The Cause of Pain Is the Association or Identification
of the Seer (*Atma*) with the Seen (*Prakrit*), and the
Remedy Lies in Their Dissociation 78

2.18. Nature Is Three Qualities (*Sattva, Rajas*, and *Tamas*),
and Its Evolutes—the Elements (Mind, Senses of Perception,
and Organs of Action)—Exist Eternally to Serve the Seer for
Enjoyment of Emancipation ,,.. 79

2.19. The *Gunas* Generate Their Characteristic Divisions
and Energies in the Seer. Their Stages Are Distinguishable
and Nondistinguishable, Differentiable and
Nondifferentiable 81

2.20. The Seer Is Pure Consciousness. It Witnesses Nature
without Being Reliant on It 82

2.21. Nature and Intelligence Exist Solely to Serve the Seer's True Purpose, Emancipation 83

2.22. The Relationship with Nature Ceases for Emancipated Beings, Its Purpose Having Been Fulfilled, but Its Processes Continue to Affect Others 84

2.23. The Conjunction of the Seer with the Seen Is for the Seer to Discover His/Her/Their Own True Nature 84

2.24. Lack of Spiritual Understanding (*Avidya*) Is the Cause of the False Identification of the Seer with the Seen 85

2.25. The Destruction of Ignorance through Right Knowledge Breaks the Link Binding the Seer to the Seen. This Is Kaivalya, Emancipation 86

2.26. The Ceaseless Flow of Discriminative Knowledge in Thought, Word, and Deed Destroys Ignorance—the Source of Pain 87

2.27. Through This Unbroken Flow of Discrimination Awareness, One Gains Perfect Knowledge Which Has Seven Spheres 88

2.28. By Dedicated Practice of the Various Aspects of Yoga, Impurities Are Destroyed; the Crown of Wisdom Radiates in Glory 89

2.29. Morals (Yamas), Observations (Niyama), Posture (Āsana), Breath Work (Prāṇāyāma), Internalizing the Senses (Pratyāhāra), Concentration (Dhāraṇā), Meditation (Dhyāna), and Absorption (Samādhi) Are the Eight Constituents of Yoga ... 90

2.30. Nonviolence, Truth, Abstention from Stealing, Chastity, and Absence of Greed for Possessions beyond One's Need Are the Five Pillars of *Yama* 91

2.31. *Yamas* Are the Great, Mighty, Universal Vows Unconditioned by Place, Time, and Class 92

2.32. Cleanliness, Contentment, Religious Zeal, Self-Study, and Surrender of the Self to the Supreme Self or God Are the *Niyamas* 93

2.33. Principles Which Run Contrary to *Yama* and *Niyama* Are to Be Countered with the Knowledge of Discrimination 94

2.34. Uncertain Knowledge Giving Rise to Violence, whether Done Directly or Indirectly, or Condoned, Is Caused by Greed, Anger, or Delusion in Mild, Moderate, or Intense

Degree. It Results in Endless Pain and Ignorance.
Through Introspection Comes the End of Pain............................. 95

2.35. When Nonviolence in Speech, Thought, and Action Is
Established, One's Aggressive Nature Is Relinquished,
and Others Abandon Hostility in One's Presence 96

2.36. When the Practitioner Is Firmly Established in Truth,
Their Words Become Potent That Whatever They Say
Comes to Realization... 97

2.37. When Abstention from Stealing Is Firmly Established,
Precious Jewels Come 98

2.38. When the Practitioner Is Firmly Established in Abstinence,
Knowledge, Vigor, Valor, and Energy Flow to Him...................... 99

2.39. Knowledge of Past and Future Lives Unfolds When
One Is Free from Greed for Possessions 101

2.40. Cleanliness of Body and Mind Develops Disinterest in
Contact with Others for Self-Gratification 101

2.41. When the Body Is Cleansed, the Mind Purified, and the
Senses Controlled, Joyful Awareness Needed to Realize the
Inner Self Also Comes 102

2.42. From Contentment and Benevolence of Consciousness
Comes Supreme Happiness.. 103

2.43. Self-Discipline (*Tapas*) Burns Away Impurities and
Kindles the Sparks of Divinity... 103

2.44. Self-Study Leads toward Realization of God or
Communion with One's Desired Deity 104

2.45. Surrender to God Brings Perfection in *Samadhi* 105

2.46. Asana Is Perfect Firmness of Body, Steadiness of
Intelligence, and Benevolence of Spirit 105

2.47. Perfection in Asana Is Achieved When the Effort to
Perform It Becomes Effortless and the Infinite Being
Within Is Reached 106

2.48. From Then On, the *Sādhaka* Is Undisturbed by Dualities 107

2.49. *Pranayama* Is the Regulation of the Incoming and Outgoing
Flow of Breath with Retention. It Is to Be Practiced after
Perfection in Asana Is Attained... 107

2.50. *Pranayama* Has Three Movements: Prolonged and Fine Inhalation, Exhalation, and Retention—All Regulated with Precision According to Duration and Place 108

2.51. The Fourth Type of *Pranayama* Transcends the External and Internal *Pranayamas* and Appears Effortless and Nondeliberate 109

2.52. *Pranayama* Removes the Veil Covering the Light of Knowledge and Heralds the Dawn of Wisdom 110

2.53. The Mind Becomes Fit for Concentration 110

2.54. Withdrawing the Senses, Mind, and Consciousness from Contact with External Objects and Then Drawing Them Inward toward the Seer Is *Pratyahara* 111

2.55. *Pratyahara* Results in the Absolute Control of the Sense Organs 112

Conclusion 113

Roots of the Yoga Sutras 115

About Erin Evans 119

About *Unraveled* 121

Glossary 123

Preface

The spell was cast the moment I walked into that Mysore yoga studio that smelled of *nag champa* and devotion. I saw golden statues of elephants and an altar at the front with a black-and-white photo of yogis of old. I watched people twice my age move their bodies in ways I could only imagine. What was this magical land?

Fast-forward twenty years, and I'm still deeply enchanted by yoga. Ashtanga yoga was my gateway in; it was rock 'n' roll and rough around the edges. It shook the fiber of who you thought you were and what you thought you were capable of.

Yoga is for the "I don't like it but I'll do it anyway" people. It breaks you, shakes you, and makes you. Regardless of your preferred style of practice, we practice yoga to support the person we are becoming. Insight without application is useless; therefore, yoga without integration is just gymnastics. Beyond the stylish yoga gear, the motivational quotes, and the sweaty forms, there is a vast ocean of teachings and information on how to access the present moment. People are compelled to practice for that sacred moment when the identity falls away and time becomes irrelevant.

Early on, teachers I revered would quote from the *Yoga Sutras of Patanjali*. I desperately wanted to understand this text, so I bought three different copies. I would make tea and sit comfortably, hoping to be transported by the words, yet each time I opened the book, I instantly felt bored. Maybe I was not smart enough or spiritual enough. Maybe *asana*, physical yoga, was the depth of it for me. Yet something inside urged me to keep trying.

This book is a compilation of all the yoga sutra translations I have read and the teachers I have studied with. This is my interpretation of the first two chapters of the yoga sutras. This is a love letter to everyone who has entered the temple of my heart: my family, my friends, my teachers, my students. I intend to shed some light on a deep, dense topic that continues to captivate my unruly attention. Let's keep it simple. Let's keep it relevant.

> "Everybody dies, but not everybody lives."
> —Drake

Sweet lover of mine.

We've been together twenty years, my god, how time flies.

You have been with me through it all. You held me when I was too weak to stand.

You loved me when I couldn't love myself. You've made me laugh out loud and cry snot bubble tears.

You've seen all my demons—the jealousy, the guilt, the competition, the self-loathing—and you still think I'm worth it.

You annoy me, agitate me, and perplex me.

You've reminded me to always see the light even when all around me darkness swirls.

I give my life to you because I can't imagine another way.

The Teacher-Student Prayer

Om saha nāvavatu
saha nau bhunaktu
saha vīryam karavāvahai
tejasvi nāvadhītamastu
mā vidviṣāvahai
Om śāntiḥ, śāntiḥ, śāntiḥ

May we be protected together.
May we be nourished together.
May we create strength among one another.
May our study be filled
with brilliance and light.
May there be no hostility between us.
Om peace, peace, peace.

The Ashtanga Opening Invocation

Om

*vande gurūnām caranāravinde
sandarśita svātma sukhāvabodhe
nihśreyase jāngalikāyamāne
samsāra hālāhala mohaśāntyai
ābāhu purusākāram
śankhacakrāsi dhārinam
sahasra śirasam śvetam
pranamāmi patañjalim*

Om

Om

I bow to the lotus feet of the supreme Guru
Which awaken insight into the happiness of pure Being,
Which are the refuge, the jungle physician,
Which eliminate the delusion caused by the poisonous herb of Samsara
I prostrate before the sage Patanjali
Who has thousands of radiant, white heads
And who has, as far as his arms, assumed the form of man
Holding a conch shell [divine sounds] a wheel [discus of light] and a sword [delusion]

A guide is a trusted person who has traveled or reached a destination in an unfamiliar area. This person can show points of interest along the journey and explain the meaning and significance of those places. The practice of yoga, as the opening mantra suggests, is paying respect to those teachers who have devoted their lives to this practice and now guide us through ours. Because of their missteps and insights gained, we start a little further along the path. We recognize that our teachers are human, and like the lotus flower that grows from muddy, dark waters, they have made mistakes and, in so doing, are waking up. The teachers who have experienced illumination and freedom from conditioned existence provide students with the firsthand experience of happiness through being. The characteristics of being human are aversions and attachments that lead to suffering. The practice of yoga is to remove that which veils who we already are. For a teacher to share what they love, they need a receptive student. The two belong together, and in their search for lightness, they are both forever changed. May we be the shoulders for others to stand on.

> "We stand on the shoulders of giants."
> —Isaac Newton

1
Samādhi Pāda Sutras

From a young age, I've been enraptured by movement. I recall watching a gymnast do a back handspring and thinking that it was the most beautiful thing I had ever seen. I wanted to embody the fluidity that I saw. My motives were clean; I didn't want accolades or anyone's approval. I was genuinely pulled by the rhythm and ease I saw in her body. I spent hours in my basement on the cement floor trying to learn this "trick." When I finally executed it without landing on my head, it was just as good as expected. Like any great discipline, the more you practice, the easier it looks and feels. My spark of interest in this "action" indicated that I had found something worthy of my attention, something important enough to dive into without wanting anything in return.

The final limb on the eight-limb path of yoga is *samādhi*. *Samādhi* translates as "total absorption and engagement with the present moment." Absorption happens when you are captivated by what you are doing and have access to a flow state. There are no ulterior motives other than the task at hand; you are all in.

Athletes call it "being in the zone"; musicians call it "the pocket"; and yogis call it "flow." This flow state is a timeless place where the ego evaporates. To be fully engaged in a moment requires curiosity, persistence, and a challenge. It elevates one above their normal worries, fears, and neuroses. It is a place of spontaneity and potentiality. There is no attachment to results and no identity. This is our highest state.

The power of this state is that once touched, it can be recreated in less intense situations. What or who calls all of you forward? We each have a role to play. *Samādhi* is about lining up with your way. We use these yoga techniques to know ourselves better and figure out how to get to God / *īsvara* / High Self, using our gifts, and personalities. Find your flow, and find your freedom. The back handsprings in my basement have led me to my beloved: yoga. This *pāda* explains that the thinking faculties of the mind are lazy because they are based on habit and momentum, not presence. Patanjali provides methods to eliminate the clouds in our minds so we can achieve clarity and feel alert.

1.1. The Practice of Yoga Starts Now!

Atha yogānusāsanam.[1]*

Yoga happens now, so why wait?

Why wait for the love of your life to tell you the relationship is over, or the doctor to say it's malignant, before you decide to change? Pain tends to be the doorway into change, yet tragedy is not the only entry point. The decision to change can be made in an instant, but it requires work. Taking your life into your own hands means getting to know what you are thinking about, how you are acting, and how you are feeling. What we practice is who we become, and much of what we practice is our past. Yoga is an invitation to cross the threshold of past to present, personal to universal, adolescence to adulthood. The transformation from experience to wisdom is in digesting stories of victimhood and sharing the learnings of resilience so the younger generations, our species, can evolve. Elevating humanity starts with you.

We control very little. What we can control are our minds and our bodies. That's where yoga comes in. *Yoga*, "to yoke," is to unite the body, mind, and spirit through breath and body. We make the impossible possible by touching our toes for the first time or falling back in love with ourselves. Yoga is about being an active participant in one's life, moment to moment.

Why is abiding in the present moment such a challenge?

The function of the brain is to keep us safe, to watch for and anticipate threats. This survival tactic has us living in the past and projecting into the future. We look to our past to determine our predictable futures and prepare for life instead of living it. This way of "autopilot living" leaves no room for spontaneity and the unknown. Yoga was created out of a need, a need for purpose and meaning. The yogis of old noticed the tendency of their minds to ruminate and rehash. They observed an undercurrent of boredom, sadness, and pain. They coined a word for this feeling: *duhkha*— *du*, "heavy and compressed," and *kha*, "space." Duhkha is what draws a person to yoga. You've come to live a big life, a heartfelt one, where there is no room for wondering "what if" when you hit the finish line. This requires courage. Open your eyes.

When the student is ready, the teacher appears.

1.2. When the Fluctuations of the Mind Stop, Yoga Happens.
Yogah cittavrtti nirodhah.[2]*

A poppy opens during the day in response to sunlight and closes at night when the insects that pollinate are dormant. The poppy knows and trusts its purpose and rhythm. Yoga is the apprenticeship of learning how and when to open and close. If one is too open, they'd feel drained and self-sacrificing. If one is too bound, they live a half-life and feel lonely. To practice yoga is to consciously choose to close off from the external world, giving one the ability to purify the thinking. This stillness and solitude supports one's ability to contribute to the community when the time is right. What is your perfect blend of solitude and association?

Nirodhah is the ability to channel and direct our thinking, moving from a busy mind to a point of focus. The field through which we experience the world is the *citta*, and it consists of three layers: *manas* ("the mind"), *buddhi* ("the intellect"), and *ahamkara* ("the ego").

The *citta* is our cognition, purpose and meaning, and motion. We are constantly navigating the ever-changing external world, and information is flying at us, demanding that we interpret, filter, and respond. When the *citta* gets caught on a snag (called a *vrtti*, or "a repetitive thought, be it a fight or a concern"), it is challenging to remove this hook and land in the present moment. This sutra speaks directly to the mind and its constant turnings. When we do not identify with the story or the fluctuation of thought, we are in a state of yoga. We direct our energy, regulate our breath, and stop the constant moving; we empty ourselves and find peace. Yoga happens when the mind field stops.

1.3. Then the Seer Dwells in Their Own True Splendor.
Tadā drastuh svarūpe avasthānam.[3*]

Below that fancy personality—your home, job title, friend group, and number in the bank account—who are you? We can spend a lifetime trying to be interesting and fit in—into societal norms, our families, our skinny jeans. We may attempt to fill time and space with money and things. But no amount of success can fill that God-shaped hole in our hearts and bring the inner peace that we are after.

The Sanskrit word *svarūpe* translates as "splendor, a brilliant appearance or color." To dwell in one's highest truth is to marvel at this remarkable body and this particular moment. It is choosing participation over perfection. Using the vehicle of the body and moving from the periphery (muscles, bones, and tissues) into the subtle body, the Inner Self can access something beyond space and time. If you were to distill the essence of "you" into one drop, what would it be? Be that. Embody your energy, so much so that people feel your presence. No need to force-feed techniques or push your agenda; be you. This part of you is free from attachment and has nothing to prove.

1.4. At Other Times, the Seer Identifies with the Fluctuations of the Mind.

Vrtti sārūpyam itaratra.[4*]

The teacher's eyes are the color of the sea. When they speak, everyone listens. They begin to discuss a background intelligence within each of us—a part of us so true and strong it can never be hurt, destroyed, or altered. This intelligence is much like a projection screen at a movie theater. The screen is blank, and we project movies onto the screen. Whether it's a romantic comedy or a thriller, the screen does not fall in love or fear for its life; the movie that is projected onto the screen does. We are continuously projecting movies, dramas, and stories onto the screen. In modern times, we are not renunciants living in caves or on mountaintops. We live in communities with families, work, and responsibilities. Being in this world requires us to experience the human joys and pains of living and loving, of hurting others and being hurt. The magnitude of our scope as humans can be overwhelming and occupy much of our mental real estate. A simple conflict could send one into a tailspin affecting their entire week and all their interactions. When we identify with our pains and dramas (our *vrttis*), we are mistaking the changing world for the pure, and in turn, we suffer. Through yoga techniques like breath work, postures, and meditation, we connect with this background intelligence.

The Sanskrit word *sansyoga* is a mix-up of the background intelligence and our human experience. Mistaking what is transient for what is permanent, we suffer. The entire point of our practice is to untangle the two so we can enter the now. This breath, this moment, is all there is.

> "Now here or nowhere."
> —Baron Baptiste

1.5. The Movements of Consciousness Are Fivefold. They Are Cognizable or Noncognizable, Painful or Not Painful.

Vrttayah pañcatayyah klistā aklistāh.[5*]

This is a setup sutra for the subsequent six that follow, and it discusses how the mind works. To untangle the pure from the impure, we must track the mind—its habits, pulls, and hooks. We must understand the nature of the instrument that creates everything we experience—our minds.

The brain is like Velcro for negative experiences and Teflon for positive ones. That means that for each negative interaction, we need nine positives to come back to neutral. What classifies a painful thought? A painful thought is based on something that has occurred in our past; it may be a limiting belief, an assumption, or an interpretation. Let's dive in.

Limiting belief—a belief you have about the world, other people, and situations that hold you back from success and stop you from getting what you want. These beliefs aren't necessarily about you, but they affect your progress:

- "Showing emotion is a weakness."
- "Successful people are lucky."
- "You have to work hard to make money."

When you realize that you have a firm belief about the world that does not support the direction you are headed, it's time to go in for surgery. We must challenge these beliefs by asking, "How true is this?" "Where did I learn this?" and "How does this belief affect me?" In so doing, we cut out the root causes of our unnecessary pains.

Interpretation—an opinion you create about an event, situation, or experience. You make up a quick story based on your beliefs and past experiences. You look for evidence to support it and believe it to be true.

When I left my former partner, my child and I moved out of our three-bedroom home and into a one-bedroom apartment. We shared a bunk bed and had one window that looked out onto a brick wall. I remember panic attacks and a mouse infestation. Did I just make the biggest mistake of my life? I was the valedictorian of my university class, and look at me now—broken, alone, and not sure how to make ends meet.

"I know," I thought, "I'll consult an expert."

The health service worker who provided free counseling services had spit bubbles in the corners of his mouth. I was desperate. This person was telling me that as a single parent, I needed to get a real job. Teaching yoga wasn't lucrative, so I should consider getting something more "stable."

"Think of your child," he said.

I was thinking that he represented all of Alberta and every professional in the world and that I should take his advice. He was rational and logical, and he did not know me.

But I'm not wired that way. I do not want to play it safe, and if I'm thinking of my child, I want to thrive doing what I love and for him to see a living example of purpose.

> "We don't see the world as it is, we see it as we are."
> —Anaïs Nin

This person, basically a stranger to me, offered up advice based on their interpretations of the world, single parents, and yoga teachers. Be discerning when acquiring advice.

Shortly after my encounter with Spit Bubbles, a friend popped by my tiny home and said, "It's like you punish yourself with scarcity. Do you not think you deserve more?"

After that moment, I changed my lens. Instead of seeing problems, I saw solutions. I longed to own a home and consulted my council: my family and friends. If I could tap into the frequency of possibility, as a single parent entrepreneur, so can you.

Look back on your life, and consider how far you've come. Continue to commit yourself to greatness—greatness in your words, actions, and the way you love. Infuse yourself into your life. Have ferocious self-accountability. Refuse to be out of integrity. Show up every day, and do your work. The key ingredient in successful people is grit—the resilience to take action.

Assumption is a belief that because something happened in the past, it is automatically going to happen again. Assumptions are personal and based on what you have experienced thus far.

Sometimes when I see "happy" families, I scoff. I see through the cracks. I see the resentment of one stifling the other. I see one keeping the peace, although desperate to be seen in a different light. I've been there, so I know. But do I?

They call it confirmation bias. It's the idea that when you believe your experience to be the truth, you will see your worldview corroborated everywhere, proving you are correct. If I believe my past depicts my future and yours, I'm living in a bleak reality and awaiting inevitable disappointment. The truth is, life is what you make it. Keep your head up and your eyes open.

> Old ways cannot open new doors.

1.6. They Are Caused by Correct Knowledge, Illusion, Delusion, Sleep, and Memory.

Pramāna viparyaya vikalpa nidrā smrtayah.[6*]

From the moment we understood and used words, we began to create our reality. Our minds took over, filling in the blanks in an attempt to understand as much as we could take in. The mind operates on autopilot, doing what it has done for centuries. The five classes of thought fluctuations are as follows: valid knowledge, error, conceptualization, sleep, and memory.

1.7. Correct Knowledge Is Direct, Inferred, or Proven as Factual.
Pratyaksa anumāna āgamāh pramānāni.[7*]

How do you accumulate knowledge and know it to be the absolute truth?

Knowledge acquisition is through our senses, which we run through our rational mind (*manas*) and what we are conscious of (*citta*). We see a red robin. Then we scan our mind for patterns and know that a robin has a red belly and they inhabit this area, so this is a red robin (*pratyaksa*). Seeing smoke in the trees, we deduct that there is a forest fire (*anumāna*). For matters that have no visible representation (a water molecule, destructive thoughts), we reference texts and people we trust. Higher intelligence (*buddhi*) is the decision-making part of the mind that processes information in an instant and is developed through contemplation, isolation, and discernment.

1.8. Erroneous Knowledge Is Based on the Nonfact, or the Nonreal.
Viparyayah mithyājñānam atadrūpa pratistham.[8*]

There is a story of five blind people who have never come across an elephant before. They find an elephant, and each person attempts to conceptualize the elephant by touching different parts: the skin, the foot, the tusk, the tail. Each person describes an elephant based on their limited experience, and the descriptions vary greatly. The moral—humans tend to claim absolute truth based on their limited, subjective experience as they ignore other people's limited, subjective experiences, which may be equally true.

> "We don't respond to what happens,
> we respond to our perspective of what happened."
> —Buddha

1.9. Verbal Knowledge Void of Substance Is Imagination.

Sabdajñāna anupātī vastusūnyah vikalpah.[9]*

Fictional books and movies are captivating with fantastical characters and adventurous plot lines. Moviemakers play to our imagination, creating worlds more vibrant than the ones we inhabit. When watching a fictitious story, we are cognizant that it is untrue, and we let our minds be pulled by the magic or violent nature of the tale. The mind, much like the playwright, creates inventive stories more enthralling—be it more dramatic or romanticized—than one's current reality. But unlike the playwright, one believes their own fabrications. Through reflection and questioning such delusions, they can be transformed into wisdom and discernment. To live in our delusions, be they appealing or appalling, keeps us disconnected from what is real.

1.10. Sleep Is the Nondeliberate Absence of Thought Waves and Knowledge.

Abhāva pratyaya ālambanā vrttih nidrā.[10]*

Yoganidrasana, the sleeping yogi pose, is from the second series of ashtanga yoga. The posture is executed while lying on the back, taking both legs behind the head, and binding the hands behind the back (super relaxing). The pose is said to relieve stress and fatigue and give the practitioner access to meditation and half sleep. A practitioner must stay calm through conscious awareness to undertake this form safely. The juxtaposition is the level of expertise and surrender required for this posture; this speaks to the intention and power behind sleep, or *nidrā*.

Of all the practices and supplements that support mental clarity and relaxation, sleep is the most important. Sleep is the mind and body's natural way of recharging, and the benefits are vast: mood elevation, willingness to meet challenges, and more energy for a wakeful time. The learning process is continuous while we sleep as memories are consolidated. During sleep, the senses of perception (eyes, ears, mouth, nose, skin); the organs of action (voice, hands, feet, organs of excretion and sexuality); and feelings come to a halt. Call to mind the image of a horse-drawn carriage. The rational mind is the driver, our desires are the horses, our five senses are the road, and our consciousness is the passenger. During sleep, there is no need to pull back on the horses' reins to draw our senses inward (*pratyāhāra*) because the passenger (the consciousness) prevails. No longer caught up in the minutia of thought, as the senses of perception and things to perceive have been suspended, consciousness merges with the mind, and the seer is experienced. This is a taste of *samadhi* (bliss) but is not the true state.

After a full night's rest, if one awakens feeling scattered or dull, it indicates the quality of rest. There are three types of sleep, and they correlate to the *gunas* (refer to sutra 1.16). After a *tamasic* sleep, one feels heavy; after a *ragasic* sleep, one feels agitated; and after a *sattvic* sleep, one feels refreshed. This indicates that through practice, one could master a preferred state of consciousness even while sleeping.

1.11. Memory Is the Unmodified Recollection of Words and Experiences.
Anubhūta visaya asampramosah smrtih.[11]*

Etched in our minds are memories, snapshots from our past. The brain encodes an experience, stores it, and later retrieves it. These impressions can be an aid or a hindrance. Through repetition, an act can become so deep-seated that it is innate within us, leading to a high level of skill and mastery. An emotionally charged memory has us narrowing our focus and acting in certain ways to prevent or recreate that same feeling. This desire to avoid pain or recreate pleasure can have us projecting our past into our futures. Paying attention to the picture in our minds assists in the development of discernment.

Discernment is the ability to judge well and make a choice. Knowing that memories are collected through correct knowledge, illusion, delusion, and sleep and can be altered through the hands of time, one must be diligent about what they believe to be true and what they wish to carry forward.

1.12. Commit to Your Practice without Attachments in Order to Still the Mind.
Abhyāsa vairāgyābhyām tannirodhah.[12]*

I'm in Miami, and the heat is on. I'm in a Mysore room led by Tim Feldmann. I make my way through the first series and move into the second. I execute *laghu vajrasana* (little thunderbolt), take a *vinyasa*, and lower to my knees for the big daddy (*kapotasana*).

Like an angel, Tim appears with the brightest blue eyes I've ever seen and says, "Today you catch your heels."

Oh gawd. Tim anchors my sacrum and takes me backward. I catch my heels. It's been more than five breaths. Have I been forgotten about? I start to panic.

After what feels like an eternity, I am lifted up, and Tim says, "*Vairāgyā*, Erin, you gotta learn to let go."

The teacher is speaking of my attitude in the posture. While in the form, I was resisting, clinging to fear, unable to let go into the moment. I wanted the form to feel different than it was, and I was creating chaos in my mind, the opposite of *nirodha*.

The Sanskrit expression *vairāgyā* translates individually as *vi* ("without") and *raja* ("desire"), sometimes referred to as "freedom." I've spent my whole life pushing, striving, thirsty for a high. Where does that addictive pattern get me? It keeps me on the hamster wheel, chasing momentary hits of pleasure and unable to just *be*. We practice yoga to become free—free from our attachments, free from the past, and free to be present. Our practice (*abhyāsa*) is our laboratory. This is our chance for a new way.

1.13. Practice Is the Steadfast Effort to Still These Fluctuations.
Tatra sthitau yatnah abhyāsah.[13]*

Have you ever stopped and observed the way the wind hits the top of a wave and although the mass of water is traveling toward the shore, that wind pulls the top of the wave back just slightly? To observe, to watch, is to give your whole attention to something beautiful; your mind must be free of preoccupations. When the mind is quiet, it is sensitive to extraordinary beauty. For a split second, you are present.

See and be transformed by what you see.

In those beautiful moments, the small self evaporates and we are left gobsmacked. Yoga is observation. It is the yearning to go home—not a physical location, but a feeling of adequateness in our own skin and in this moment. It is the realization that no amount of money, coffee, or episodes of Netflix can fill the void. It is the desire to find contentment from moment to moment regardless of any situation or outcome.

To the untrained eye, these forms might appear like perfectionism or exercise. In reality, they are about mastery. Yoga is mastery over the senses, the body, and finally, mastery of the self. *Mastery* is defined as "the possession of great skill and technique." It is prowess, dexterity, proficiency, and genius. Mastery is about showing up again and again. Each time you step on the mat, you are given a choice: evolve or remain. If you remain the same, everything repeats, the storms endure, the lessons stagnate. Yoga is a reset. It won't be easy, but it will change the game for you. You will explore what lies outside your comfort zone.

1.14. Long, Uninterrupted, Alert Practice Is the Firm Foundation for Restraining the Fluctuations.

Sa tu dīrghakāla nairantarya satkāra āsevitah drdhabhūmih.[14*]

Yoga practice starts out as a love affair. You sneak away on your lunch break or before work; you come back glowing. It's private and personal, secretive and seductive. Nothing it says or does offends you. You've finally found your missing puzzle piece. Over time, like a relationship, you begin to see its demands. The physical pain, your laziness, and all the other choices seem more appealing than rolling out your mat. What is required of you in your practice is commitment. A commitment is a promise, a firm decision to do something. This pledge, or vow, is to focus on one thing with devotion. Saying yes means saying no to all other options. Commitment is risky, and there is no promise of any particular outcome. It's risky because there is exposure, vulnerability, and the possibility of hardships or maybe even failure. So why bother? Committing is going deeper. It's an invitation to discover what you are made of. It allows you to see your patterns of avoidance, aversion, and distraction. Without commitment, we play it safe, we dip our toes in, we keep our options open. Treat your commitments with a sense of wonder and excitement.

> "What you seek is seeking you."
> —Rumi

1.15. Renunciation Is the Practice of Detachment from Desires.

Drsta ānusravika visaya vitrsnasya vasīkārasamjñā vairāgyam.[15]*

Each time we bow in a yoga practice, we are bowing to the person we want to become. We are accepting the challenges of our sacred work to eliminate our attachments and our clinging. We are lining up with "the way" because we care deeply about our short time on this planet. To renunciate is to keep only what is necessary. We empty out and simplify so we can align with our High Self. We study our daily actions to determine what brings us closer to the light and what takes us farther away. On the mat, we create momentum that filters through every corner of our lives. Through discipline, we attune our bodies and minds to possibility and mystery.

Your practice is at the core of your evolution. Who do you want to become, and what must be dropped to attain that?

To be devoted is to practice with an earnest heart and a sense of pride in your forms. Each posture is a chance to show up as your best and offer it up with no hopes of reward or recognition. The postures become offerings for your altar. Our practice brings us close to our godliness, where separation disappears and stillness reigns. Hearts pounding, lungs expanding, muscles stretching—a place to come to and attempt to live from. A quest for humility and kindness, where the ego falls away and we are one.

1.16. When One Gains Knowledge of Spirit (*Purusa*), They Cease to Thirst for the Manifestations of the World (*the Gunas*).

Tatparam purusakhyāteh gunavaitrsnyam.[16]*

As mentioned in the introduction to the *Yoga Sutras* (p. 2), the Samkhya school of Indian thought is dualistic, meaning the world is made up of *purusa* ("soul, pure consciousness") and *prakrti* (that which is created in manifest form). There are three *gunas* that are said to make up the manifested world of *prakrti*:

1. *Tamas* is slow-moving, heavy, sedated energy. It is inertia—think of getting sleepy after eating too much Thanksgiving dinner; lethargic, "drag yourself out of bed" moods; and not being able to stop yourself from binge-watching your favorite TV show.
2. *Rajas* is activity, productivity, and knowledge (albeit perhaps a bit ungrounded). Think of going to war against a to-do list in a coffee-fueled buzz, getting pumped up to go after your goals, and listening to Tony Robbins every morning to motivate yourself to be super productive.
3. *Sattva* is equanimity, lightness, and flow. Think about the zone of genius that artists get into; the "high" you get when you forget that you exist while flowing through asana practice and everything just feels "right"; and the moods you get in where the world seems perfect and you can only see the good in people. It's not forced/delusional optimism but a genuine knowingness that everything is exactly where it needs to be, right here, right now.

Everything in the world is said to be made up of these *gunas*, these energies. When it comes to our spiritual development, it is useful to remember that even our thoughts, emotions, and actions are manifestations of the *gunas* as well. Instead of a "black-and-white," three-category system, think of them as points on a spectrum that goes up or down. Lower energies tend to be more *tamasic*; middle energies tend toward *rajasic*; and higher energies are more *sattvic*. Beyond *sattva* is a state beyond individual experience that can glimpse the vastness of pure consciousness: *purusa*.

Once one intimately knows the unbounded oceanic freedom of spirit in this way, nothing else compares. Like a kid who tries chocolate ice cream and no longer wants to eat his vegetables, the seeker who tastes the purity of consciousness will no longer yearn for the emotions or manifestations that come from the energy of the *gunas*; it simply cannot compare.

Don't try to outright reject the *gunas* when you begin your journey—the "ultimate detachment" that exists through knowing consciousness can just be tamasic apathy disguising itself as being spiritually profound or detached—when in reality, you're just too lazy to care about anything. That isn't spiritual—it's self-deception!

Instead of trying to skip steps and become detached from the *gunas* all at once, look at your thoughts and emotions closely. What is the energy behind them? Some emotions may not sound very "spiritual," but they are stepping-stones to the more profound, higher states of *rajas* and *sattva*. True spiritual realization is awareness of your inner world; there are no wrong feelings on the way there.

1.17. Practice and Detachment Develop Four Types of *Samādhi*: Self-Analysis, Synthesis, Bliss, and Experience of Pure Being.

Vitarka vicāra ānanda asmitārūpa anugamāt samprajñātah.[17]*

There are two sources that drive the mind and our lives: energy (*prana*) and desire (*vasana*). We wake up in the morning with our desires and use our energy to act upon those desires. Some desires lead to more peace and ease while others lead to burnout and dissatisfaction. Yogis use their physical bodies to direct energy and learn about their desires. To master the mind is to understand what it already does and use that to our advantage. The four ways the mind can access flow (*samadhi*) are through conjecture, enjoyment, I-am-ness, and contemplation.

- *Vitarka* ("conjecture, argument"). Considering all options, write lists of pros and cons and compare one thing against the other. On the mat, we use our conjecture by noticing and directing what our senses take in: hot/cold, up/down, right/left.
- *Vicāra* ("reflection/observation"). This watchful quality of the mind observes and listens. This is the capacity to sense and connect. On the mat, we imagine we are watching ourselves move and breath.
- *Ānanda* ("enjoyment, bliss"). Our modus operandi is to pursue pleasure throughout the day. By studying our re-

lationship to bliss on the mat, we can find an inner spaciousness within our postures that allows more depth and presence. The word is often loosely translated as "bliss," but in truth, it means "accepting what is ordinary."
- *Asmitā* ("ego, I-ness"). The ego, our sense of I, allows us to show up and be in the world. The flaw of the ego is that it can become enlarged or made minuscule. We are attempting to move from the small self, which is alive but not permanent, to the High Self, which is ever present and uncontaminated. To use the sense of I-ness within your practice is to put your personal stamp of approval on each of your forms. A yogi uses their physical body to understand the universe and all that is sacred. You are the owner of beautiful. Be a rebel and trust your own aesthetic. Stay woke, stay wild.

Trust what you love.

1.18. The Void Arising in These Experiences Is Another *Samādhi*. Hidden Impressions Lie Dormant but Spring Up during Moments of Awareness, Creating Fluctuations to the Purity of Consciousness.

Virāmapratyaya abhyāsapūrvah samskārasesah anyah.[18]*

I cut myself not with razor blades but with my inner dialogue. I open Instagram and see perfect bodies and happy couples:

"You are not enough." Slice.

My child cries, and I get angry instead of tender.

"You are a bad parent." Stab.

I berate myself for being human, and nothing is ever good enough. I fight this sensitivity with toxic positivity:

"Be grateful."

"It could be worse."

I examine my flaws and mask them as "growth." This way of looking outside myself to find myself is like looking at an image of the earth and mistaking that for the earth. I am so much more than this bag of bones. I am joy, presence, and love. What is this story costing me? Everything. Connection, love, and inner peace. The pain is too much, and the cost is too high. I am ready to end the cycle of abuse. This is my story, and yours is likely in the same category on Netflix—an epic tale of self-loathing, comparison, and hustle.

Just as the power and flow of the river grooves through the rocks it passes over, our thoughts weave grooves in our brains. Repetition creates an easier path for our thoughts to travel, making it difficult to think of new things.

Samskāra translates individually as *sam* ("complete") and *kāra* ("making or action"). *Samskāra* is the harmful way the mind repeats and acts on momentum and autopilot. The way we worry and ruminate is often out of habit and no true reason. To wake up or to become conscious is to bring what was in the shadows into the light, to become aware of thoughts that have been driving our lives and be brave enough to choose a different way. To experience something new, we must do something we have never done.

The word *pratyāhāra* is "the process of pulling back on the five senses in order to go inward." All saints, sages, and gurus tell us to go in. They wouldn't tell us to do it if it wasn't a good idea. To go inward is to slow down long enough to catch old *samskāras*. The "I'm not good enough," the "I don't have what it takes," the "why does this always happen to me?" programs have been running the show for a long time. Through yogic purification, no rock is left unturned.

1.19. In This State, One May Experience Bodylessness or Become Merged in Nature. This May Lead to Isolation or to a State of Loneliness.

Bhavapratyayah videha prakrtilayānām.[19]*

The quest for consciousness is a continuous journey. We learn the repetitive, unconscious nature of our minds and how to go beyond thought to a compelling place of stillness. All that being said, there are those born into this world with powers beyond our comprehension. These folks know *prakriti*, the material world, and they embody it. They become one with nature—be it water, air, earth, or fire. For a moment they become bodiless and one with *prakriti*. Their skill is beyond us, but their practices have led them here. The difficulty with this absorption is that it is not the final destination, and the practitioner may get stuck here and never truly become free.

1.20. Practice Must Be Pursued with Trust, Confidence, Vigor, Keen Memory, and Power of Absorption to Break Spiritual Complacency.

Sraddhā vīrya smrti samādhiprajñā pūrvakah itaresām.[20]*

Being a yogi can be lonesome because as you put your conditioned ways of being into question, people and habits will fall away. The above sutra speaks to the five allies, or friends, the yogi must keep close if they are to progress on the path of yoga.

- *Sraddhā* ("faith, trust, reverence")

Faith is your metaphorical ace in the hole. It supports you when your dreams are unorthodox or audacious. Faith is the antidote to anxiety and insecurity. But faith must be cultivated. Slowly, patiently, complete trust, or confidence, is built by practice and holding oneself accountable. It's about following through and being consistent even when you don't feel like it. The flip side of faith is doubt. In Buddhism, questioning the teachings and the teachers is encouraged and termed "skillful doubt." For doubt to be skillful, we have to be close enough to a subject to care about it yet open enough to let the questioning come alive. Skillful doubt brings us closer to the truth. Unskillful doubt is the opposite and is synonymous with cynicism. Cynicism is self-protective and allows one to feel smart and unthreatened without really being involved. A cynic can look sophisticated and remain safe. A cynic sits on the sideline and complains. One who possesses skillful doubt gets their hands dirty. Each time you succeed, you build your faith bank account. Faith builds trust.

> "Those who are certain of an outcome can afford to wait and wait without anxiety."
> —*A Course in Miracles*

- *Vīrya* ("strength, energy, vigor")

Natural talent only goes so far. It's determination and vigor that take one beyond the crowd. Determination is the act of coming to a decision or settling on a purpose. Determination is the bloody fingers from strumming the guitar, the late nights writing, the blistered feet from running, the relentless trying in the pursuit of your purpose. Purpose is the long game, the impact of one's actions; it's undeniable knowing that doing the thing is better than not doing the thing. On the mat, as we progress, we tend to plateau. We do not have as many breakthroughs, and therefore it might not feel as rewarding. In truth, the practice is all smoke and mirrors; we think we are getting somewhere by crossing postures off our list when, in reality, we are flexing the muscle of concentration and commitment. This grit is about getting command of your mind so you can choose things that are for your own best interest that create outcomes that pay you back, return on investment (ROI). It means delaying that instant gratification. Study your habits and routines; get honest about your pain and your joys. Will this path lead you to the promised land, or are you headed to a detour?

- *Smrti* ("memory, recollection")

Have you ever tried to learn guitar? At first your fingers stumble, you hit the wrong strings, you forget the chords. But after some time, the chords become familiar, your fingers dance on the strings. As your memory of the chords becomes better, you can add more difficulty to the music you play. Yoga is like this. We learn the basics of the forms: where to put our feet and hands, when to inhale and exhale. After a while we become more proficient at the forms and begin to add another layer, the locks (*bandhas*), the gazing point (*dristhi*), and the binds. This element of memory allows us to land in the postures more quickly and accurately, giving us the opportunity to land fully in the moment.

In the primary series of ashtanga yoga, we are introduced to *bakasana* (crow pose). Having built the strength through many *chaturangas* (low push-ups), we have the muscle memory to support our body weight on our hands. Our proficiency in the forms builds through memory. In the third series, we find *urdhva kukkutasana A*—wherein we enter a tripod headstand, tangle our legs in lotus, lower our lotus to the back of our arms, and pick our head up. The memory of what was required in *bakasana* (crow) feeds into our aptitude for *urdhva kukkutasana A*.

- *Samādhi* ("absorption, enthrallment, devotion")

This entire first chapter is based on this word. Let's break it down: *sama* ("balanced, perfect"), *dhi* (from the world *dyana*, which is "mediation or concentration"). Often explained as complete absorption in the task at hand, *samadhi* is a full investment of your attention. It is the movement from mediation to the final stage which is poise and attention.

- *Prajna* ("awareness of real knowledge acquired through intense contemplation")

Mahatma Gandhi was a freedom fighter for India. A highly educated person and deeply immersed in social change, Gandhi led India to independence from the British rule in 1947. Incarcerated eleven times and treated with violence and hatred, Gandhi always responded with peace and passive resistance. When asked about his time in prison and the inhumane treatment he received, Gandhi said, "I will not let anyone walk through my mind with their dirty feet." This commitment to nonviolence was built through years of reflection, patience, and practice. Awareness of one's moral code is not acquired through books or teachings alone; it is through consistent contemplation and self-questioning. The action is in the reaction.

1.21. The Goal Is Near for Those Who Are Supremely Vigorous and Intense in Practice.

Tīvrasamvegānām āsannah.[21]*

"You're too much."
"You think?"
These words pierce sharper than a knife. If you have ever been told this, I hope you took it as a compliment. There are intrinsic and extrinsic motivations for all things. Intrinsic is your personal stoke; extrinsic is the external world telling you they approve. Do it for you: the art, the music, the yoga.

For those with a fierce passion to live their yoga, it might feel as though the rest of the world is moving in slow motion. You might be tempted to mute yourself, play small, or fit in, but Pantajali states that for those with intensity and enthusiasm, the access point to *samadhi* is closer.

> "Sometimes it takes darkness and the sweet confinement of
> your aloneness to learn. Anything or anyone that does not
> bring you alive is too small for you."
> —David Whyte

A toast to the black sheep, the rebels, to those who love with totality and no reservations, to those willing to be all in or not at all, to those making their dreams come true and refusing to let their music die inside. A toast to the brave souls with scars on their bodies and their hearts, to those who took big risks that others couldn't fathom. Remember, you risked it all because you have faith. To the single parents with your invisible capes, I see you.

Only those people, places, and things that are for our highest.

1.22. There Is a Difference between Those Who Are Mild, Average, and Keen in Their Practices.
Mrdu madhya adhimātratvāt tatah api visesha.[22]*

A student of mine is very proficient at handstands. People assume it was easy for her and that by some stroke of luck, she was gifted with an aptitude for weight-bearing on her hands. Truth is, she is nearly six feet tall and has worked very hard and thoughtfully to get to this place. The fellow yogis marvel at these physical capabilities, but what I marvel at is this student's consistency, studentship, and attention to detail. The handstand is irrelevant, and she knows it. Her physical practice has been the gateway to presence and channel for her life force. What this student's fellow yogis can't see is her persistence, failures, and reverence. This student is humble and available. She practices with a clear head and a keen heart; because of this, she has control over her desires, mental quietness, and supreme detachment.

All that being said, the world needs all types of practitioners, and depending on where you are in your life cycle—child-rearing, sick children, aging parents, building businesses—your intensity of practice may look different. No matter the kind of yogi you are (mild, medium, intense), you have an awareness that is above ordinary human standards. If you have heard the call, lucky you.

- *Mild*—has developed an intellectual analysis at an external level; will be able to differentiate between knowledge and mental alertness.
- *Medium*—has knowledge of bliss and the Self.
- *Intense*—has control over their desires, ceasing of brain fluctuations, mental quietness, and supreme detachment.

1.23. The Mind May Be Restrained by Profound Meditation and Surrender to God.

Īsvara pranidhānāt vā.[23]*

The word *God* can be confronting. It might conjure up images of you in uncomfortable clothing sitting on a wooden pew at Sunday school. Perhaps you were taught that God is vengeful and we are all sinners. But the word *īsvara* does not translate directly as *God*, but rather, "chief suitor, owner of beautiful, High Self." In the context of the sutras, *īsvara* is the watchful force that is unconditionally loving and ever present. Poetry is often used as a bridge to describe this indescribable force. We've heard that God made man in God's image, and yet many of us use man and make it God's image: punitive, uncaring, conditional. The qualities of God are unconditionally loving, wakeful, and profound goodness.

> "The sharpest sword will not pierce it;
> the hottest flame will not singe it;
> water will not make it moist; wind will not cause it to wither; it is vast, perfect and all pervading, calm, immovable, timeless."
> —*Bhagavad Gita* 2.23

Pranidhānā is "the fixing of attention, prayer, or bowing to." It's the decision to give yourself up to this great yearning for connection and Self. We offer our practice up—each asana a prayer, each breath a mantra. We put our stamp of approval on every form. The only promise of the practice is inner peace. By practicing with a devotional quality, we place a vote on ourselves rather than leaving our lives in the hands of fate.

1.24. God Is Untouched by Conflicts, Actions, and Cause and Effect.

Klesa karma vipāka āsayaih aparāmrstah purusavisesah Īsvarah.[24]*

Karma is a pillar of Buddhist thought, and many people get turned off by Buddhist philosophy when they feel that karma is used as an explanation for why bad things happen, children starve, or people get sick. When I refer to karma, it's related to my personal actions and the equal and opposite reactions/consequences of those behaviors. When my motives are not truly in service, the net karma balance shifts. An example, I speak ill of a friend behind their back, and now I feel guilty. To make up for this, I go out of my way to be kind. I am attempting to right my wrong. The first action is bad. The second action is good but motivated by a selfish desire for absolution, and therefore the penance detracts from the goodness of my deed.

Karma is the law of cause and effect: every action has a counter and equal reaction, a price, a theoretical cost. My ill will toward my friend results in me wanting to put in the effort to feel better about my bad behavior. My desire for forgiveness is true, but there is an energetic cost to fixing my first bad action. By understanding our intentions, we practice improved decision-making when the choice to inflict harm is presented. If we are guilt-ridden over a negative behavior, the cycle of affliction is exasperated and guides our aspirations for forgiveness/absolution. In an attempt to balance that karma, we offer good behavior, but the feelings of shame and misappropriated trust are left still, and the scales do not level out. To use karma to justify things we cannot explain (starving children) is to place the onus on the living thing's previous life's karma.

Bad things happen for no reason, and it hurts; our action is in the reaction. How we respond to a negative event or situation is the measure of our character and the real reflection of our karmic intention. Reflecting on our own and others' behaviors and motives is different from overthinking and should be considered as part of a holistic understanding of oneself.

Dharma is the Sanskrit word for "justice or virtue" and is about living on purpose. It is a life driven by head-and-heart connection and alignment. Purpose is not always a massive undertaking, like saving the turtles; it can be smaller and closer to home. It's the way you live and how you communicate. It is your quest to feel more alive and to shift from the self to the collective. The word *purpose* is defined as "the reason for which something is done or created." It is about the method behind one's madness. It is the why, the ambition: the family dinners and folded laundry, the sweaty workouts and mountains climbed, the five-o'clock wake-up calls. It's feeling wrecked and showing up anyway.

1.25. God Is the Unexcelled Seed of All Knowledge

Tatra niratisayam sarvajñabījam.[25]*

When my child was born, the energy of love in the room was palpable. Seeing this baby's scrunched-up face and tiny fingers was the closest thing to God I had ever seen. I felt cradled. The force that has animated my child's first breath is the same force that animates myself, the trees, and you reading this now. This force decides when we take our first breath and when we take our last one. This force is ever present, ever powerful, and ever knowing.

1.26. God Is the First, Foremost, and Absolute Guru, Unconditioned by Time.

Sa esah pūrvesām api guruh kālena anavacchedāt.[26]*

The Greek philosopher Socrates said, "Know thyself." Socrates spoke of wisdom being acquired through knowing what you do not know and that your true nature is an immortal soul. This is the practice of yoga. Using the physical practice of movement and breath, one discovers what lies below the surface of the body, the mind. Through meditation, the realization hits—that we are not the thoughts that swirl but something timeless and present. Through practice, we build the capacity to linger in this state of peace. To live as though a part of you will live forever is to act with care, accountability, and sustainability.

You are stardust and magic. The God we speak of lies inside. Stop outsourcing your power by looking for a savior, a lover, a teacher. Be wary of false idols selling you something they say you need. The moment you believe God is outside of you, you suffer. There is a part of you unbroken. Get familiar with that part, and question everything.

> "If you meet the Buddha on the road, kill him."
> —Linji Yixuan

1.27. He Is Represented by the Sacred Syllable *Aum*, Called *Pranava*

Tasya vācakah pranavah.[27]*

We cast spells with our words, painting our realities with what we say. To speak up is to say what we mean and have people listen. Yet we live in a culture that wants us to lie just a little. That's how we protect each other, right? When telling an untruth, our spirit recoils, pulls back, or hides. Chanting is clearing the cobwebs from our truth, teaching ourselves the power of our own voices and words. The word *mantra* consists of two words translated as *man* ("mind") and *tra* ("to free or protect"). To chant the sacred sound *aum* is to access a higher brain wave and to strategically choose where we put our attention.

> "Raise your words, not your voice."
> —Rumi

1.28. The Mantra *Aum* Is to Be Repeated Constantly, with Feeling, Realizing Its Full Significance.

Tajjapah tadarthabhāvanam.[28]*

In yoga, we use repetition as a way to get present and face monotony. Our intention is to take the mundane and make it sacred. The repetition (*japah*) of the sound of *aum* is intended to help us recognize that we are not our bodies, our successes, or our personalities; we are love. It is a simple and devotional sound. By chanting *aum*, we are connecting with the part of us that is reverent and faithful.

1.29. Meditation on God with the Repetition of *Aum* Removes Obstacle to the Mastery of the Inner Self.

Tatah pratyakcetana adhigamah api antarāya abhāvah ca.[29*]

I'm lying in *shavasana* after an epic yoga class in San Franciso next to a person I hope to one day call my second partner in marriage. The teacher asks us to rise to our seats for a sea of *aums*. At this point on my journey, I am not super into *aums*, but I have drunk the Kool-Aid and am feeling the vibe. We are to begin our *aums* with the teacher and then follow our own breath and timing and will collectively decide when the sea of *aums* is complete.

I close my eyes and chant this auspicious word again and again. I feel the energy in the room rising and feel a connection to each student. It is as though I am above my body, watching; we are no longer separate beings with bodies but a collection of vibration and love. Jealousy and competition do not live here. Time dilates, and it feels like only a moment has passed. After the sea of *aums* is over, we sit in silence, the death of the sound, the calm after the storm.

Aum is a call to be liberated from the confines of the human body, mind, and ego. It consists of three parts that make up the entire universe, the triad of divinity: Brahma the creator, Vishnu the sustainer, and Shiva the destroyer. Everything has a life cycle: the trees, the waves, the human life. The moment of creation is the spark (*a*); a sustained life is growth and living (*u*); and in the end, everything must die, like my relationship with that person next to me (*m*).

Using this mantra, we remove the obstacles to the mastery of Self.

1.30. These Obstacles Are Disease, Inertia, Doubt, Heedlessness, Laziness, Indiscipline of the Senses, Erroneous Views, Lack of Perseverance, and Backsliding.

Vyādhi styāna samsaya pramāda ālasya avirati bhrāntidarsana alabdhabhūmikatva anavasthitatvāni cittaviksepah te antarayāh.[30]*

Each person is born into the world with their own set of preferences, interpretations of beauty, and gifts to offer the world. This uniqueness of sight is what gives the world dimension and variety. As a seeker, our job is to uncover what it is that lights us up. The Sanskrit word *vasana* translates as "our greatest wish or desire."

Yoga is a practice to discover everything that prevents, blocks, and impedes us from getting close and staying close to our greatest aspiration. The road to our calling is scattered with obstacles, and we must remove each one with care and kindness. The obstacles, however big or small, need to be studied and understood if we are to remove them and keep them at bay.

The room is hot and sweaty. We have just finished two hours of Mysore yoga practice, followed by an hour of *pranayama*. Our bodies worked, our minds clear and calm. The teacher sits at the front of the room, putting a collared shirt on over their sweaty Ganesha tank top. They seem unaffected by the heat and show no signs of fatigue after waking up at 4:00 a.m.

Our next session is on the nine obstacles. This teacher pulls out a picture of a Hindu demigod. They explain that demigods are said to be half human, half god and that they have reached a divine state after death. It is said that demigods watch our progress, and when they feel we are getting closer to our *vasana*, they throw down an obstacle in hopes of steering us off course. These obstacles have the power to knock us down and back into slumber. By going back to sleep, we go back into the suffering. What is required when hit by an obstacle is to dig deep and persevere in order to stay on the path.

The first obstacle is *vyādhi*, "sickness or injury." A car accident kicked me out of my home. I shattered my ulna, dislocated my elbow, had stitches in my head, and got a severe concussion. This accident had me questioning everything I thought I knew. With the thing I loved the most taken from me—my practice—I felt raw, angry, and confused. I had FOMA (fear of missing asana). Who was I without my practice?

I did heal. With a lot of physiotherapy and patience, I recovered. I still feel the metal in my arm, my eyes are sensitive to light, and noise can overwhelm me. With injury or illness comes a depletion of energy. The visceral experience of pain makes inspiration difficult. When our immune system is down, it requires us to rest. This forced break in practice or work can inevitability impede our momentum. It requires verve to return to your previous capacity and output. One must study their pain, its source, and recognize what must be done to heal it. This sickness may be physical or mental.

If you are injured or ill, do your work to get strong and healthy. Get back on your feet again. The world needs your art.

Did you know your brain releases serotonin, similar to a high from drugs, when speaking about ideas? That release of hormones is why people get addicted to talking about ideas versus following through with them. Dreaming up ideas feels as good as cocaine, in theory. In contrast, bringing ideas to life is grueling. With any dream and its coming to fruition, there will be red tape, there will be mistakes, and there will be stress.

The second obstacle is *styāna*—"apathy, or a loss of interest." It is the feeling that an area of your life is unworthy of your attention. When it hits, you feel like giving up. You wonder where the spark went and whether you even liked it in the first place. Loss of interest can show up in the physical body and the mind. This feeling of inertia can be present in practice or in the care of your finances. Its pull is powerful and ultimately is an avoidance of what needs to be done. We are creatures of action and are always acting. Where are you putting your efforts? Television, social media, substances, socializing? This unhelpful busyness takes us away from the joy and our sacred blueprint. Our work is to be engaged and alive in our lives, every corner, every facet. Look in your metaphorical junk drawer for all the places in your life where you feel apathetic. Apathy, like depression, feels like a burden too big to deal with, so you hit the Snooze button and roll over. It is a part of the human condition. The good news is, it doesn't have to be that way, and after confusion, clarity comes.

Keep coming back to the why—the intention behind your ideas, your practice, and your life. Showing up on good days is easy, but how about on the hard ones? Focus on one idea, and make it your life. Think of it, dream of it, live on that idea. Let your brain, muscles, nerves—every part of your body—be full of that idea, and leave every other idea alone. That is the way to success.

Don't let the process drain you. Don't let rules or money or the will of others push you into forgetting. You love what you love because it drives you. It makes you feel alive, and that spirit is contagious. That feeling is the most real thing there is and the closest thing you're ever going to get to capturing the essence of the universe. It's lightning, it's fire, it's passion, it's truth. It's a kiss between two strangers that changes everything forever.

"I am inadequate, insufficient, not enough"—perhaps the deepest of human fears. Inadequacy feeds on the belief that our inner resource is not to be trusted. We build fancy veneers to distract the world from seeing that we believe we are not enough. By building strong bodies and acquiring impressive knowledge and material, we feel in control and the world applauds us. This, however, is not the depth we seek. *Ampleness* is knowing that what is ours will always be ours. Building a strong body, gaining knowledge, and being successful is incredible, and while you do so, stalk the monster of inadequacy.

The third obstacle is *samsaya* ("doubt"). It is expressed threefold: doubt in oneself, doubt in the teacher, and doubt in the teachings. Self-doubt comes from a belief that although born perfect, we have somehow become flawed while living. Self-doubt has us looking outward to find out where we fall on the spectrum of lovability and importance. There is no guardian at the gate admitting only the worthy ones in; you are the custodian of confidence.

Everything you need is inside of you; the rest is smoke and mirrors. Trust yourself. Be honest, and investigate how you shape your words, thoughts, and actions. Self-esteem and efficacy are the remedies to doubt. Self-efficacy is a firm commitment to who you want to become and reorganizing your life to become that.

In the beginning, it's so easy to care. You are enthralled and notice the subtleties. After a couple of months or years, the object of your affection—be it a person, a hobby, a job—loses its magical pull. You become slightly withdrawn and less attentive.

The fourth obstacle is *pramāda*, or "carelessness." Yoga is a great place to observe carelessness. We practice the same forms every day, and that could sound boring; but to a yogi, it is our laboratory. We show up happy or sad, injured or healthy. We study our pain, breath, body, and the present moment.

The fire is lit. You've made big commitments. You'll read a chapter a day, practice five days a week, drink celery juice. One morning you wake up tired, lazy, and not in the mood. You give yourself a pass. You can read two chapters tomorrow. Then one day off becomes two, then three.

The fifth obstacle is *ālaysa*, "physical laziness, the avoidance of activity or exertion." Believe me, no one's situation makes it easier for them to do the work. All of us have bad days, sore days; the point is, we show up. To be human is to have multiple dispositions. Relationships, work, finances, and physical pain all impact how you feel in the morning. Knowing this allows for some kindness to yourself on days you feel off. When you feel off, show up anyway, but show up in a different way. Stick to your commitments; the fire burns brighter each time you do it. Commit to your discipline. Know that the practice is designed to combat laziness.

Our desires drive our lives. They dictate what we are drawn to and determine the direction of our lives. However, when a desire comes from the expectation of a reward or an avoidance of emotion, we must consider whether it is in our best interest. There is nothing wrong with a drink, a smoke, or a shag, but if you are attempting to regulate inside emotions with outside stuff, that's a problem. If sense objects are drawing you away from your drive, discipline, and devotion, check in.

The sixth obstacle is *avirati*, "the desire for sense objects." Turning to unwholesome things to feel whole creates mind activity and more of what you don't want. Check your attachments. Are your habits supporting your life?

You have one precious life; how do you want to live it?

In an externally driven world that focuses on comparison and materialism, practicing yoga is an act of rebellion. Yoga asks the practitioner to go inward. To shut oneself off from the distractions of the world to discover a vast landscape that is undisturbed and limitless. The practice of yoga is to pull apart the material, cyclical world from that which is never changing and always present. To mistake the impure for the pure is to attach eternity to that which is transient. Our bodies, our family, and our friends live and die; to pray they will never leave or change is to mistake the temporary for the permanent. In doing this, we create attachment and suffering for ourselves.

The seventh obstacle, *bhrāntidarsana*, is "living under an illusion." The remembrance that life is fleeting reminds us to live it well. Don't be afraid of bright colors, loud noises, risky decisions, sudden changes, or even failures. Enjoy your moments and your people; do things that scare you. The art of letting go is the art of living well.

Why do you do what you do? To provide for your family, to follow your passions? What starts out clear can become muddy when the attention and money flow. We can get sidetracked. A business person attempting to create stability for their family can get caught up in riches and neglect the family. An actor who acts for the love of the art can get more interested in the fame and lose the flame.

The eighth obstacle is *alabdhabūmikata*, "missing the point." When we confuse the dangling carrot for our goal, we create patterns of grasping and competition and might find that while our bank accounts are full of green, our hearts are full of greed. When one becomes ensnared by this obstacle, it is like mistaking the brick and mortar of the temple for God himself.

Stay steadfast in the pursuit of what you love.

I'm in the Mysore room, and I'm working second series and part of the third series. I get to *durvasana* (leg behind the head standing up), and I feel like crying . . .

"This is hard. Maybe I should get a real job, work nine-to-five at a bank, cut my hair, and marry a person from the bank named Patrick who refuses to go by Pat. We could send each other cute little interoffice memos and have a kid who is afraid of germs."

And then I hear that little voice inside my head that says, "You will change this world with your own two hands."

I'm not gifted with numbers or mortgages, so the bank is not my calling. I'm gifted with people and movement. I guess I'll stay put.

The ninth obstacle is *anavasthitatvāni*, and it translates as "the inability to maintain achieved progress." With a new level of performance comes a new level of faith and efficiency. You feel overwhelmed by what is expected of you and unsure of whether you have the *prana* to maintain it. To remain at this level requires clear vision and momentum. Give your life over to something bigger than you.

1.31. Sorrow, Despair, Unsteadiness of the Body, and Irregular Breathing Further Distract the Citta.

Duhkha daurmanasya angamejayatva svāsaprasvāsāh viksepa sahabhuvah.[31*]

A shaman asks, "How's the weather?" This person is not asking about the atmospheric pressure or the temperature but rather what is going on inside the mind and in the body. Our bodies, breath, and emotions are incapable of lying and therefore reveal when we are distracted. It is our due diligence to weed out our mental gardens and observe where we are out of alignment with our path. The four indicators that we are out of alignment are sorrow, despair, irregular breathing, and unsteadiness of the body. The following eight sutras speak about controlling these interruptions and their symptoms.

1.32. Adherence to Single-Minded Effort Prevents These Impediments.

Tatpratisedhārtham ekatattva abhyāsah.[32]*

I did it again. I looked at my ex's Instagram. The person who put my heart in a blender.

They call it digital cutting. I see his smiling face with his new love, and they look happy. The parasitic mind kicks in: "I am not enough." "The new partner is better." "I do not deserve love." I wallow for some time and then take action to shake myself out of this delusion. The Sanskrit word *ekatattva* translates as "one truth."

Truth with a capital *T* is an accepted worldview: the world is round, there are four seasons, and Elvis Presley is the greatest artist of all time. Small-*t truth* is our perception of what we see based on limited information and our pasts. *Truth* is who you really are; *truth* is who you think you are. When in the throes of sorrow, a yogi can take it upon themselves through practice to choose a more productive point of focus, to grab one principle and stick to it—perhaps the sound of your exhale, your thumb gaze. In this case, I took myself for a bike ride and enjoyed the beauty of nature. The Truth is that nature is amazing; nature does not prefer a jaguar to a bacterium. Every part of nature is important, and there is no hierarchy. Him loving her is irrelevant to me loving me.

1.33. We Must Have Friendship for All. We Must Be Merciful toward Those That Are in Misery. When People Are Happy, We Ought to Be Happy, and to the Wicked, We Must Be Indifferent.

Maitrī karunā muditā upeksanam sukha duhkha punya apunya visayānām bhāvanātah cittaprasādanam.[33]*

Plastered on T-shirts. Tattooed across skins. It's that four-chambered, blood-pulsing muscle we associate with love.

But . . .

What is love? Is it romantic or parental? Is it unconditional or with caveats? Is it eternal, or can it be withheld on a whim of "if you don't behave the way I want you to"?

Love is truth. It has no checklist of standards that can never be met. It is not a score sheet and is not to be earned. Love is in the details. To be cracked open by love is an invitation. This is what we came here for. Eventually, you won't need the falling in and out of it to feel it. It is everywhere.

Yet . . .

We guard our hearts. Overschedule, judge, criticize, exclude, plan, gossip, and control—all in hopes of protecting that which is most sacred: our hearts. This sutra speaks to the four abundant qualities of the heart, the ways we close it, and how to make a different choice.

When there is happiness (*sukha*), greet it with friendship (*maitrī*).

When we feel happy, there is a tendency to mistrust how long it will last, and therefore, we may brace ourselves for the next bad thing. We are urged to teach ourselves to gravitate toward sweetness. This is a remembrance to lean in when you feel spacious and happy. It is a kind and friendly attitude toward oneself. On the yoga mat, notice if the mind becomes preoccupied with the final destination of a posture rather than enjoying the space you are occupying.

Explore your joy, and increase your availability to it.

When there is pain (*dukha*), greet it with compassion (*karunā*).

Guan Yin is the goddess of mercy, the embodiment of compassion. When Guan Yin was preparing to exit the material world, she stood at heaven's gates and heard the cries of suffering on earth. At that moment, she realized her work was not done and decided to stay on the human plane until all suffering was alleviated. In her right hand, she holds a vase of water, signifying the nectar of life, and in her left hand, a willow branch symbolic of flexibility and indestructibility. Compassion is the realization that we are one and that our pain unites us. To be compassionate is to hold discomfort without trying to fix it or numb it. It is the understanding that pain shapes us and that within each of us is the power to handle and transmute it. Life is working for us, and each situation we face is grace.

Do you want to be a vehicle of pain in the world or a vehicle of peace?

When there is virtue (*punya*), greet it with joy (*muditā*).

While most people have sight, not everyone has vision. Vision is the long game, the seeing of the playout of your actions before you act. It is the foresight to act in accordance with your own moral compass regardless of who is watching or what the merit will be. With kindness, a ripple of kindness flows through the world; with anger, a ripple of anger. To live skillfully is to free oneself from incurring more karmic debt. When you are virtuous, honest, and honorable, celebrate by bringing awareness to a job well done and thus create momentum in that direction.

The Sanskrit word *muditā* translates as "an unselfish joy for the good fortune of others." What a heartwarming concept—Disney should write a movie script about it. Lack mentality has us competing for resources, assuming another's success is inevitably our loss. Jealousy is a powerful emotion that closes the heart and has us acting rigidly. When a neighbor, friend, or colleague is successful, can we feel it as though it was our own? Start small, in places that it feels true. To bring awareness to the shadow of competition is to call what is hidden into the light.

> "If you want to become whole, let yourself be partial.
> If you want to become straight, let yourself be crooked.
> If you want to become full, let yourself be empty.
> If you want to become reborn, let yourself die.
> If you want to be given everything, give everything up.
>
> The master sets an example for all beings
> Because he doesn't display himself people can see his light.
> Because he has nothing to prove, people can trust his words.
> Because he has no goal in mind, everything he does succeeds."
>
> —Lao Tzu

When there is immorality (*apunya*), greet it with neutrality (*upekshanam*).

We are all trying to navigate life as best we can, and sometimes we falter. We cheat, we lie, we hurt the people we love, we fall short on our commitments, and it makes our skin crawl. When you act out of alignment, you will likely blame or criticize yourself. When facing a transgression, approach it with neutrality. To be neutral is to be neither for nor against. This is not numbness or toxic positivity but rather space for reflection and integration.

How about when others falter—they lie, cheat, or hurt us or the ones we love? How quickly we armor up, choose sides, cancel, exclude, villainize to keep that perpetrator away from us. This polarizing tactic of separating can feel safe, and if the memory lives on inside your heart, it is not effective. Forgiveness does not mean what they did was right, but it lets you off the wheel of suffering.

> "Can you love the person but hate the act?
> Can we oppose evil without getting caught in righteousness and good?"
>
> —Ram Dass

1.34. Or by Maintaining the Pensive State Felt at the Time of Soft and Steady Exhalation and during Passive Retention after Exhalation.

Pracchardana vidhāranābhyām vā prānasya.[34]*

We come into this world and take our first breath, and before we exit, we take our last one. This is our very connection to life, and we rarely observe, study, or play with it. A big pillar of the yoga practice is breath work. To land at the top of an inhale and be full or linger at the bottom of an exhale and be empty requires great attention and care. This method of retaining the breath helps to calm the mind.

1.35. Or by Contemplating an Object That Helps to Maintain Steadiness of the Mind and Consciousness.

Visayavatī vā pravrttih utpannā manasah sthiti nibandhanī.[35]*

> Where attention goes, energy flows.

The practice of yoga is learning to flex the muscle of concentration. It begins by placing your eyes on one particular spot for five breaths. Over time it builds to knowing exactly where to place your hands, feet, eyes, and the timing of your breath. The first stage of accessing concentration is by placing your attention on one object: an image, a candle, the sound of *aum*. Choosing the object of one's attention and staying with it brings steadiness and ease to the mind.

A *vrtti* is "an automatic unconscious thought on repeat." It is reactive like lust, anger, revenge, or being right. When a practitioner begins to see the harmful nature of their patterned mind, they realize that there are other choices available.

A *pravrtti* is "an evolution, or change in thought from a negative to a positive." It is consciously choosing a different thought.

Nivrtti is one step beyond this and requires mastery. *Nivrtti* is "neutrality or abstinence from a thought." Using our practice and discipline, we rewire our brains because we understand there is a higher knowing beyond thought. This higher knowing is our power center, our freedom. Although bound by a body and responsibilities, we are free to choose.

1.36 Or Inner Stability Is Gained by Contemplating a Luminous, Sorrowless, Effulgent Light.

Visokā vā jyotismatī.[36]*

If you've crawled your way out of some imaginable experience, you now know what you are made of. Once the story has been processed and no longer belongs to you, you can pull the curtain back on the issue and be transparent. That is how you change the world—not by reading books or attending seminars, but by looking into your own human suffering. Adversity reminds us that pain is everywhere and we control very little. Sorrow is a part of the human mind, and it is easier to hold on to than joy. Yet the deepest part of ourselves is untouched by karma and drama, and it is the seat of our soul. It does not operate on time or memories but on deep knowing. To go inward and contemplate this light, the practitioner learns to stay motionless and thoughtfully silent.

1.37. Or by Contemplating on Enlightened Sages Who Are Free from Desires and Attachments or Divine Objects.

Vītarāga visayam vā cittam.[37]*

An altar is a sacred mantel to place items that spark reverence: a candle, a picture of your teacher, a deity, a lock of hair from your ex. On the mat, each posture becomes an offering to the altar. We step onto our mats with a busy, distracted mind (*cittavikshepa*), and through the heat of the practice, we shift our distracted minds into a reverent, blessed state of mind (*cittaprasade*). This state of mind is our truest state and has one point of focus.

On my altar sits a picture of Indra Devi, a practitioner who brought yoga to the West. Indra was a professional dancer from Europe and became intrigued by yoga. Indra showed up in India with a heart condition and begged Krishnamacharya to teach her this ancient practice. Krishnamacharya refused based on Indra's gender and the laws at the time. Indra was persistent and pure of heart. Through their networking abilities, Indra became friends with the king, and with the king's blessing, Krishnamacharya began teaching Indra yoga. After years of diligent study, Indra returned to America to share yoga with as many people as she could.

Each morning before practice, I light my candle, look at Indra's face, and sit in silence contemplating the commitment, faith, and verve Indra had for the practice of yoga.

1.38. Or by Recollecting and Contemplating the Experiences of Dream-Filled or Dreamless Sleep during a Watchful Waking State.

Svapna nidrā jñāna ālambanam vā.[38]*

Yoga philosophy predates psychology, and much of what the yogis talked about was later discovered by psychologists. An example is Austrian psychologist Sigmund Freud's three levels of mind model. Freud established that the mind consisted of three parts: the conscious mind (10 percent), the subconscious mind (50–60 percent), and the unconscious mind (30–40 percent).

The conscious mind is that which we are aware of (the reflection of the moon on the water). The subconscious mind is the storage of memories for quick-recall, automatic actions that we do without thinking because we are skilled (riding a bike, jumping through to seated). And the unconscious mind is the storage of past events and memories that we cannot access (the first time we laughed). Yogis added one more level of the mind: the superconscious mind, which is *samadhi*.

If our intention is to access this superconscious state—total absorption—we must understand the levels of consciousness. When sleeping, the senses are naturally restrained; therefore we have an easier entry point into the intelligence of our minds. To reflect on our dream space (*svapna*), which may seem out of our control, is to glean insight into the subconscious mind. To decipher the wisdom of both the dream state of consciousness (*svapna*) and the dreamless state of unconsciousness (*nidrā*) is to experience an inner reality that does not require any validation. One must distinguish between fantasies unfulfilled and what is useful for enlightenment. Upon going to sleep, a practitioner should contemplate the soul.

The way we see determines what we see.

1.39. Or by Meditating on Any Desired Object Conducive to Steadiness of Consciousness.

Yathābhimata dhyānāt vā.[39]*

I remember the guide's hands, tanned and weathered from fishing. A silver ring was on their middle finger, and its contrast against their skin was mesmerizing. We spent a summer working together in northern Saskatchewan at a fishing lodge: Arnold, a guide, me (Erin), and a dock person. Arnold taught me to cast, catch, fillet, cook a fish, and drive the boat. They shared their culture with me, no holds barred.

That was one of the most impactful summers of my life. Arnold was one of the most influential people I had met. He told me to find beauty everywhere I went (in the clouds, in the landscape) and to always notice something new—in another, in myself, in the world. That summer I was introduced to space and silence. At the end of the summer, Arnold gifted me with an eagle feather. I am not someone who keeps much, but the one thing I have held on to for these past twenty years is that feather. My child always says, "When you die, all I want is that feather." At nine, my child understands the significance of that gift.

A feather isn't just something that falls out of a bird; it means much more. The feather symbolizes trust, honor, strength, wisdom, and power. Many indigenous people believe that if they are given this feather, it is a symbol from above. The eagle is a messenger from the Creator. Eagles are at the top of the food chain; they rule the sky. An eagle has the ability to see two miles away and can therefore spot its prey while hovering above. For these reasons, the eagle is a symbol of freedom, power, and transcendence. As one becomes more well versed in living, they are able to learn from their mistakes, failures, and successes. The symbolism of the eagle shows how powerful one becomes when they develop the ability to pan out and take a good look at their lives, seeing the triggers and patterns of their suffering.

> "Yesterday I was clever so I wanted to change the world.
> Today I am wise so I am changing myself."
> —Rumi

1.40. Mastery of Contemplation Brings the Power to Extend from the Finest Particle to the Greatest Particles to Infinity.

Paramānu paramamahattvāntah asya vasīkārah.[40]*

The first time I saw someone do a press handstand, I was in awe. If that was possible for them, it ought to be possible for me. I huffed and puffed, and nothing happened. I showed up every day and tried regardless of no obvious progress. Many years later, I did it. I effortlessly floated up and held that beautiful beast. It's not about the press handstand. It's the perseverance, the focus, and the mastery. For myself, the doorway into presence was through the physical. Now in each form, each seat, I sense my vastness and my insignificance. Yoga removes the veils and allows the practitioner to see what is right in front of their eyes.

1.41. The Yogi Realizes That the Knower, the Instrument of Knowing, and the Known Are One, Himself, the Seer. Like a Pure Transparent Jewel, He Reflects an Unsullied Purity.

Ksīnavrtteh abhijātasya iva maneh grahītr grahana grāhyesu tatstha tadañjanatā samāpattih.[41*]

The clouds roll in, the rain falls, the rain stops, the sun shines, the sky clouds over, and the snow comes. We are not the weather patterns but the vast, deep blue sky. The material world is cyclical: a seed is planted, it germinates, bears flowers, then returns to the soil from which it came. To identify with the life, death, and cause-and-effect nature of life is to cling to what is ever changing. In clinging to what was, we carry the residue of our pasts into our presents. When the momentum of habit and knowing stops, we can see what and who is directly in front of us, light a jewel, pure and translucent.

By focusing on the external rotation of our front hip in *trikonasana* (triangle pose) we train the mind to move from a clouded, active state to one that is clear, reflective, transparent, and clean. *Samapatti* is a simultaneous occurrence when everything lands as one: the perceiver, the object of perception, and the process of perception. When *samapatti* occurs, we see what is directly in front of us, not believing or projecting onto it.

1.42. At This Stage, Called *Savitarkā Samāpatti*, the Word, the Meaning, and the Content Reblended, and Become Special Knowledge.

Tatra sabda artha jñāna vikalphaih sankīrnā savitarkā samāpattih.[42]*

Traffic was crazy, and now I'm late. I hope they haven't locked the door. I rush in, toss my clothes on the bench, and run into the studio. I throw my mat down mere moments before we start. The teacher begins us in child's pose. To the naked eye, it would appear I am nailing my child's pose, but the truth is, I'm still worried about my unattended wallet and my sketchy park job. My mind is busy, elsewhere, but I've been doing this long enough to know that no amount of thinking will prevent my wallet from being stolen or getting a ticket for my parking. I'm here, so I might as well be here. I use the techniques. I focus on the length of my breath, the direction of my hands, the lift of my pelvic floor.

This is dramatic, but whether you race to class or arrive calmly, the likelihood of carrying your day to the mat is high. In sutra 1.17, we are introduced to the word *vitarkā*. *Vitarkā* means "analytical thinking used to build concentration for the moment we are in." As a new practitioner (ten years or less), we use our thinking faculties to rise above our busy minds and land in the now. This sutra goes one step further (*savitarkā*) and suggests that at some point, conjecture is no longer needed and words and language don't enter the mind. We are absorbed and become totally engrossed with the task in front of us.

1.43. In *Nirvitarka Samapatti*, the Difference between Memory and Intellectual Illumination Is Disclosed: Memory Is Cleansed and Consciousness Shines without Reflection.

Smrtiparisuddhau svarūpasūnya iva arthamātranirbhāsā nirvitarka.[43]*

Yogic philosophy is rich with myths. Myths use supernatural events and metaphors to explain the human experience.

Durga ma is a beautiful Indian goddess with long, flowing hair and a nose ring. The fact that her hair is down indicates that she is not domesticated, and the nose ring signifies her steadiness and rule-abiding nature. She rides a lion and has ten arms, and each holds a weapon in case the necessity to slay arises—what a badass.

In one myth, Durga ma begins to churn the entire ocean, and the ocean becomes silty and murky. She does not do this to be destructive but rather to bring what was stuck up to the surface. Much like the effects on the ocean, the yoga practice churns the practitioner. We begin to see where we are stuck, have played small, and have settled for less. We see our *samskaras* ("physical patterns") and our responses based on habits that cause karma more pain. These first responses are out of memory: *smriti* ("deep grooves of behavior that are not in our best interest"). Catching an automatic response gives us the ability to change it from a negative habit to a positive one.

My feet are flat, and early on teachers urged me to lift my arches. Yeah, yeah, but what about a headstand? Over time I realized that my flat feet were affecting my practice. I began catching and focusing on the pattern to change it. Now my arches lift without thinking about it. *Savitarkā* is using brainpower to create a positive change (in this case, lifting my arches), and once the new pattern is ingrained, we go beyond it to a state of *nirvatarkā*, in which there are no words or labels.

Memory (*smrti*) can often be false and feed into thoughts of shame or ill will. To be truly alive is to meet each moment as it is. This requires purifying our memories and excavating that which does not serve.

1.44. The Contemplation of Subtle Aspects Is Similarly Explained as Deliberate or Nondeliberate.

Etayaiva savicāra nirvicāra ca sūksmavisayā vyākhyātā.[44][*]

To create beauty is an act of devotion—whether at home, through art, or at work. Yet many of us rush through our days incapable of stopping long enough to notice or create beauty. To participate in life, one must act—make coffee, phone a friend, light a candle—and this first action happens through analytical thinking (*vitarkā*). After the action is complete, the mind gets quieter and more subtle. We become reflective, insightful, and contemplative; the Sanskrit word for this is *vicara*. This quality of softening and reverence is how we transform the mundane mind into one that is sacred and blessed. To go beyond logistics and inference is to have symbolic sight and patience. As the mind becomes more refined and deliberate, we transcend even this contemplative nature to a state that is free from memory, the past, karma, and drama. This state known as *nirvicāra samapatti* is a state of bliss and pure Self.

1.45. The Subtlest Level of Nature (*Prakriti*) Is Consciousness. When Consciousness Is Dissolved in Nature, It Loses All Marks and Becomes Pure.

Sūksmavisayatvam ca alinga paryavasānam.[45]*

Written inside an acorn is the blueprint for an oak tree. For an acorn to grow into a mighty oak tree, it requires the proper conditions, cultivation, nurturing, and environment. Much like the acorn, within each of us is the spark to attain self-realization, and given the right circumstances, it is possible to do exactly that. At the most subtle layer, the human being is consciousness. Our work is to dissolve the small self into consciousness through cultivating a calm mind with meditation, yoga, breath work, and nurturing our connection to source through scripture and teachings. When a practitioner realizes they are not their thoughts and bodies, they can move through the world and its constant fluctuations with a full-hearted acceptance of what is.

> "A glacier stream doesn't fight to get the river,
> gravity takes it there."
> —Ally Bogard

1.46. The States of *Samādhi* Described in the Previous Sutras Are Dependent upon a Support or Seed and Are Termed *Sabīja*.

Tā eva sabījah samādhih.[46]*

The states of absorption mentioned thus far are dependent upon *prakriti* (the material world) and are therefore seeded. A seed by its nature germinates and produces fruit. The *samadhi* that relies upon something external for cognitive blending produces more seeds, more karma. *Sabīja* is the use of cyclical matter as a crutch to assist in the concentration of the mind. A yogi might use the breath, a mantra, or a posture to teach the mind to dwell on one thing (*bīja*) and access a flow state.

1.47. From Proficiency in *Nirvicāra Sampatti* Comes Purity. *Sattva*, or Luminosity, Flows Undisturbed, Kindling the Spiritual Light of the Self.

Nirvicāra vaisāradye adhyātmaprasādah.[47]*

While inversions and twists calm our nervous systems, nothing compares to harnessing the power of our minds. To utilize the power of the mind is to understand that our biology and biography are not our destiny. This will require study, reflection, and contemplation. When a yogi understands suffering and karma, they can go beyond the limits and self-actualize. Using repetition in practice, we go beyond the ordinary. We transcend rationality and contemplation (*vicara*) and land right here, right now, pure and receptive.

1.48. When Consciousness Dwells in Wisdom, a Truth-Bearing State of Direct Spiritual Perception Dawns.

Rtambharā tatra prajñā.[48]*

I am riddled with hypocrisy. I can hold a handstand for two minutes, but I shrink at the thought of disappointing you. I am the life of the party but live for quiet nights alone. I preach nonviolence but eat meat. These contradictions make me question my authenticity. How can I be two opposing things? And if I am, does that make me an impostor, a fraud? Being human means being diverse. Our highest calling is to figure out the flow of our own lives and to figure out what blocks us from spirit—the part of ourselves that is untouched by time, pain, grief, and anger. This flow is how we get close to God. We must become still and give space for what lies inside. Wisdom (*prajna*) comes through our own experiences.

1.49. This Truth-Bearing Knowledge and Wisdom Is Distinct from and beyond the Knowledge Gleaned from Books, Testimony, or Inference.

Sruta anumāna prajñābhyām anyavisayā visesārthatvāt.[49]*

There is a point on one's journey where there is no need to lean into tradition or teachers anymore. The insight, once the mind is purified, comes from within. Look to nature and its rhythm—the seasons, the cycle of the moon, day and night, the elements.

1.50. A New Life Begins with This Truth-Bearing Light. Previous Impressions Are Left Behind, and New Ones Are Prevented.

Tajjah samskārah anyasamskāra pratibandhī.[50]*

Several years back, I was in a scrambling accident. I fell fifty meters down the front of a mountain. I broke my nose, hand, and front tooth. I had stitches on my head and legs. I recall waking up in the hospital screaming from a nightmare of falling off a cliff. For several months afterward, when I saw mountains, I would imagine falling down them. My family urged me to move homes, and many people reminded me of how dangerous mountain activities are. I felt the collective fear and my instinct to contract. Eight months after the accident, I decided to face my fear. I packed my bag and retraced my steps up that rocky, exposed peak. When I was almost at the summit, I began to weep, my heart started to race, and my body started shaking. I felt as though I could not trust myself to get to the top without harm. I slowed my breath, my pace, and my thoughts. Step by step, I made it to the apex and back down to the base safely.

Since that day, I have continued my mountain adventures and am not afraid of exposure. This story is exemplary of my refusal to let the past create my future. A *samskāra* ("a scar") is a habitual pattern of thought based on past experiences and repetition. Because of repetition, a *samskāra* becomes the autopilot of our minds and gains traction and credibility. My accident created a belief that I could not trust myself and that mountains were dangerous. I could have spent my whole life avoiding (*dvesa*) mountains and danger because that is safe. I, however, knew that to live like that would have been a contracted state. Each thought, we have a pull. To clean up our thoughts is to figure out where we are living unconsciously, preprogrammed. Over time, with care and attention, even when acting, we no longer create more reactions, and the cycle of karma comes to an end.

1.51. When the New Light of Wisdom Is Also Relinquished, Seedless *Samādhi* Dawns.

Tasyāpi nirodhe sarvanirodhāt nirbījah samādhih.[51]*

Most of us are living in consumeristic cultures that applaud personal success and individual goals. This attitude of self-preservation has us competing for resources and feeling alone. Living for results is keeping life at an arm's distance, pushing away what is unpleasant and reaching for a sense of gratification. The practice of yoga is to unlearn strategies of self-protection and learn to engage with what life presents. In sutra 1.46, we were introduced to the concept of *sabīja*, which is "to bring our attention to one point using a support such as breath, or a mantra." Once this state of deep concentration is achieved, the crutch of an external element is no longer necessary, and we access a state of *samadhi* that is without seed, *nirbīja*. This seedless attention is free of cause and effect and is not tied to any outcome. To get off the wheel of consumption and competition is to enter the field of possibilities. This entire pāda is devoted to unraveling our suffering so we can be in the moment. *Samādhi* is our way out of cemented self-perception and past victimization. *Samādhi* is our way to freedom.

"You have been telling people that this is the eleventh hour.
Now you must go back and tell people that this is the hour!
And there are things to be considered:
Where are you living?
What are you doing?
What are your relationships?
Are you in right relation?
Where is your water?
Know your Garden.
It is time to speak your truth.
Create your community.
Be good to yourself.
And don't look outside of yourself for a leader.
This could be a good time!
There is a river flowing very fast.
It is so great and fast that there are those who will be afraid.
They will hold on to the shore.
They will feel that they are being torn apart,
and they will suffer greatly.
Know that the river has its destination.
The elders say that we must let go of the shore,
push off into the middle of the river,
keep our eyes open,
and our heads above the water.
See who is in there with you and celebrate.
At this time we are to take nothing personally,
least of all, ourselves.
For the moment that we do,
our spiritual growth comes to a halt.
The time of the lone wolf is over.
Gather yourselves!
Banish the word struggle from your attitude
and your vocabulary.
All that we do now must be done
in a sacred manner and in celebration.
We are the ones that we have been waiting for."
—The Elders, Oraibi, Arizona Hopi Nation

2
Sādhana Pāda Sutras

Yoga is a practice. A practice with no upcoming game or performance, with no promises of any particular outcome. To repetitively do one thing is to gain proficiency. The yogi is not interested in competition; they are interested in mastery. Mastery is intrinsically motivated and is a continual drive to be the best version of oneself. Yoga may appear to be merely physical, but real skills acquired through practice are determination and resilience. The yogi faces failures on the mat every day. One does not attempt a headstand and then deem themselves a failure if they fall; they continue to show up and trust the process, knowing that the headstand is not the point. The yogi's response to failure is curiosity. What starts out as personal practice bleeds into all areas of the yogi's life: relationships, parenting, vocation. The practice teaches one to accept what is and play with the boundary of what could be.

Begin again, and again, and again

In the West, the streets are peppered with yoga studios. This rise in popularity makes yoga a household name. Many associate yoga with postures and breath, and this is partly true. *Hatha yoga* is the umbrella term used for physical yoga. The *Hatha Yoga Pradikipa* states that hatha yoga consists of four things: *asana*, *pranayama*, *mudra/bandha*, and *samadhi*.

- *Asana.* The word that follows each pose in yoga is *asana*—which is "seat," "shape," or "to halt." To land in a posture is to stop the movement of the body and mind.
- *Pranayama.* It is the practice of breath extension and control. Some breath techniques increase or decrease the temperature of the body; some calm or excite the mind.
- *Mudra/Bandha.* A *bandha* is a lock, gained through muscular engagement and mental focus. A *mudra* is a symbolic gesture or attitude. Every posture and transition has an attitude, and that attitude is yours to choose. Using the locks, we contain our experience inside of us uncontaminated. The postures are irrelevant; the way you do them is everything.
- *Samādhi.* The final limb of the eight-limb path of yoga is a euphoric state of meditation. This experience comes through self-forgetting and ultimate surrender.

Like a mountaineer standing upon the summit of a mountain, holding their ropes and pitons and knowing those tools were necessary for the climb but so too were their courage, perseverance, faith, and aloofness from company, we ascend to the top of the mountain (*raja yoga*) using the four tools of *hatha yoga*.

Raja yoga is defined as "supreme yoga, union through concentration of the mind, and living out the eightfold path which is yet to come" (sutra 2.29). Through practice we close off our senses to the external world and dive into our bodies and minds, which offer a magnitude of information. We see our drive for success, our laziness, our fear, our sadness, our power. Discipline is a commitment: showing up happy or sad, injured or healthy, and using compassion for both self and others on the hard days.

2.1. Burning Zeal in Practice, Self-Study, Study of Scriptures, and Surrender to God Are the Facts of Yoga.

Tapah svādhyāya Īsvarapranidhānāni kriyāyogah.[52]*

Effectiveness tends to be our standard of success, yet yogic philosophy tells us to choose faith over effectiveness. Effectiveness is tied to the outcome; faithfulness is following our own authentic path. To be faithful requires one to perform all duties with a pure heart, without attachment to the reward. As yogis, we have many duties. We have a duty to our practices, our family, our work, our friends, our bodies, our children, and our country.

Kriyā yoga is defined as the yoga of action. The yoga of action consists of three parts: *tapas, svādhyāya*, and *īsvarapranidhānā*.

Tapas is defined as "the heat created through fierce discipline." It is the monastic vow to go inward while the world is calling our attention outward. Through consistent practice, we learn the patterns and fluctuations of our own thoughts. Using the heat of our practice, we sift through our desires, removing those that distract us, so we can connect with our highest call—the imprint of our soul. We use our *vinyasas* ("breath linked with movement") and our postures to create heat; we place our eyes on one spot to focus our attention (*drishti*). We practice seriously but do not take ourselves too seriously.

Self-study, *svadhyāya*, is both the study of self and the study of scripture. To study oneself is to understand how anatomically a body does a twist and then how "this" particular body does a twist. We go beyond the physical to observe our aversions to the twist and our desires for a different twist. We take it all in, the beautiful and the confusing. Seeing oneself is understanding the human predicament of clinging to that which is not real, the past or the dreamed-up future. Studying poetry, myths, and ancient texts on God (*īsvara*), we feed ourselves with the remembrance that we are that—made in the image of God, a reflection of godliness. We are not our thoughts; we are the energy behind them. The word *pranidhānā* translates as "bow, surrender, or offer up." We are giving our efforts up to something bigger. In the context of the sutras, it is *īsvara*. *Īsvara* is one's own perception of the divine.

2.2. The Practice of Yoga Reduces Afflictions and Leads to *Samādhi*.

Samādhi bhāvanārthah klesa tanūkaranārthasca.[53]*

Through *kriyā yoga*, we go inward. We act and see the afflicted way we perceive our reality. Once aware of our suffering, we can reduce it and perhaps remove it to reach a state of profound meditation.

> "The Creator gathered all of Creation and said, 'I want to hide something from the humans until they are ready for it. It is the realization that they create their own reality . . .'
> The eagle said, 'Give it to me. I will take it to the moon.'
> The Creator said, 'No. One day they will go there and find it.'
> The salmon said, 'I will bury it on the bottom of the ocean.'
> The Creator said, 'No. They will go there, too.'
> The buffalo said, 'I will bury it on the Great Plains.'
> The Creator said, 'They will cut into the skin of the earth and find it even there.'
> Grandmother Mole, who lives in the breast of Mother Earth and who has no physical eyes but sees with spiritual eyes, said, 'Put it inside of them.'
> And the Creator said, 'It is done.'"
> —Hopi Elder

2.3. The Five Afflictions Which Distort Consciousness Are Ignorance, Ego, Pride, Aversion, and Fear of Death.

Avidyā asmitā rāga dvesa abhinivesah klesāh.[54]*

In the story of Buddha (Siddhartha), Buddha's family did not want their child to experience pain or suffering. They built walls around their kingdom to keep potential harm out. They supplied only the best food and toys. Although given everything, still Siddhartha wondered if there was more. Late one evening when the guards were asleep, Siddhartha snuck out and went into the world. The poverty and violence, the sadness and corruption, were overwhelming and perplexing. Siddhartha did not want to run back to the kingdom but rather to understand this suffering. Legend says that after studying the causes of suffering for many years, Siddhartha went into the forest, sat under a Bodhi tree, and meditated until he achieved enlightenment. To be enlightened means to be awake, aware, and present.

> "Now, he thought that all these transitory things have slipped away, I stand once more beneath the sun as I stood as a small child. Nothing is mine. I know nothing. I had to smile. Yes, his destiny was strange, he was going backwards, and now he stood empty and naked and ignorant in the world, but he didn't grieve about it. No, he even had a great desire to laugh. To laugh at himself. To laugh at this strange and foolish world."
> —Siddhartha

The causes of our suffering (*kleshas*) corrupt our seeing, and they are ignorance, ego, desire, aversion, and clinging to life. The story of Siddhartha illuminates the intention of spiritual practice: to loosen our grip on our identities and question our beliefs. What thoughts and actions lead to feelings of separation, inferiority, superiority, anxiety, and depression? The *kleshas* point us in the direction of our freedom.

2.4. Lack of True Knowledge Is the Source of All Pains and Sorrows whether Dormant, Interrupted, or Fully Active.

Avidyā ksetram uttaresām prasupta tanu vicchinna udārānām.[55*]

The Kayapo Tribe in the Amazon rainforest has a ritual. They cut and scar the face of a tribe member each time that person experiences an emotional trauma, such as the loss of a child, abuse, or illness. They also scar their shoulders each time they have been loved. The scars let others know what they have endured, and through this, their community can begin to understand and be compassionate. Imagine if we wore our scars to show our pain. How differently we might see and treat one another.

Based on ethnicity, socioeconomic class, profession, sexual orientation, and gender (to name a few), the mind labels and ranks people. It happens subconsciously and is based on our values, personal experiences, and the culture we were raised in. This way of interpreting the world is shallow and leads to othering each other. To judge a person based on their veneer makes it impossible to connect, let alone consider what they have been or are going through. Navigating the world in this superficial way leads to separation and hatred in the heart.

> "It's either love or it's not."
> —Ryan Belder

Ignorance is a lack of knowledge and information (*avidā*). To show interest in only your narrow range of experience and expertise is fertile soil for casting ideas and others away, keeping your scope limited. This first force of corruption is the birthplace of the others. *Avidyā* (or "ignorance") consists of two words: *a* ("not to") and *vidyā* ("see"). To bring what was hidden into the light requires listening and space to be wrong. The *kleshas* may be dormant, alive, or hidden.

Our pain and shame, joy and love unite us. Each scar, visible to the eye or not, is part of your legacy. I'll show you mine if you show me yours.

2.5. Mistaking the Transient for the Permanent, the Impure for the Pure, Pain for Pleasure, and That Which Is Not Self of the Self—This Is Called Lack of Spiritual Knowledge.

Anitya asuci duhkha anātmasu nitya suci sukha ātma khyātih avidā.[56]*

My underwear drawer is immaculate, each pair folded perfectly. I do not have one single sock that does not have its rightful pair; my closet is organized by color. And yet . . . that does not change my father's diagnosis. It does not help my friend grieve her mother. It does not take that baby's cancer away. If only life were as easy to organize as my home. When the walls feel like they are closing in, and the pain is too much to handle, I reach for something—a person, a handstand, a glass of something strong and dark—and for a moment the distraction helps.

Why is change so scary?

As the seasons change and the deciduous trees lose their leaves, we are not offended because we trust the seasons. Why then do we grip what was so tightly when the world around us changes—people die, house prices increase? Life is cyclical; all things have a birth, life, and death span. To release our grip on what we cannot change gives us freedom. By mistaking the impure for the pure, we place our faith in what withers and dies. *Avidyā* is "not seeing." Change is the flow of life. Change is an adjustment, a revision, a remodel.

Love can end. People we love die. Our bodies will fail us. We can lose our jobs. Friends can leave. Trauma will change you forever. And you got to: you got to love, you got to live.

> "Don't grieve, anything you lose comes back
> round in another form."
> —Rumi

2.6. Egoism Is the Identification of the Seer with the Instrumental Power of Seeing.

Drk darsanasaktyoh ekātmatā iva asmitā.[57]*

You may never know the impact you have. The words you've spoken that opened a door for a friend in need. The bridge you've built between two strangers, changing their worlds forever. That spark of passion you have lit inside a heart that saved someone's life. The way you listen and ask the right questions, never making it about you. You move through the world with care and attention, conscious of every heart you hold. Sometimes it's heavy, but you make it look easy.

> "Start a huge foolish project like Noah.
> It makes absolutely no difference what people
> think of you."
> —Rumi

Who are you?

Your appearance, job, home, likes, dislikes, achievements, failures, memories, and experiences give you a sense of "I" (*asmitā*) and distinguish you from another. Your ego—sense of I—is deeply woven into your desires, wishes, and purpose. Having an ego allows one to confidently show up and remain on target. The underbelly of the ego is how desperately it clings, and in clinging it is defensive, comparative, and competitive. An unhealthy ego has two sides: overly boastful or self-deprecating. Identifying solely as ego, we are caught in spiritual ignorance (*avidyā*), mistaking our power for God's power.

May we pull back our identities, roles, and letters behind our names in order to connect with one other and this moment. Stay curious, stay open.

2.7. Pleasure Leads to Desire and Emotional Attachment.
Sukha anusayī rāgah.[58]*

An eating disorder stole much of my youth. I found yoga, and the craving and controlling stopped. I was saved—praise Jesus. Instead of considering what my body looked like, I marveled at what it could do. This is the slippery slope of our human condition. We drop one addiction and promptly pick up another. I became profoundly attached to the form, the next one, and the next one. To be attached to anything—a person, a pose, a youthful body—is to give it your power. Your attention is your most powerful commodity, so choose wisely where to direct it. Desire (*rajah*) drives our attention. We seek pleasure, satiate it, and then hunger for more. Pleasurable experiences ignite more desire and attraction, which creates attachment. Attachment leads one to become absorbed in the pursuit of pleasure and addicted to the sense of gratification. Desire is important and powerful as it directs one's life, but we must study our relationship to pleasure with a fine-tooth comb.

2.8. Unhappiness Leads to Hatred.
Duhkha anusayī dvesah.[59]*

Dvesa translates as "aversion or hatred." It is natural to dislike tasks, and it is important to do some things you do not love. You may not love exercise, yet it is important for the health of your heart. You may not like administrative duties, yet it is important for the health of your business. On the mat, we face our aversions, be it backbends, forward-folds, or breath work. Facing our dislikes on the mat reveals how much of our efforts go toward pushing away what we do not like. If we are interested in growth, our opinions must be fluid. With experiences and maturity comes an unraveling of what has been taught, modeled, and believed to be true. All hatred leads to unhappiness.

Do you want to be right, or do you want to be free?

2.9. Self-Preservation or Attachment to Life Is the Subtlest of All Afflictions. It Is Found Even in Wise Men.

Svarasavāhī vidusah api tatha ārūdhah abhinivesah.[60]*

When my child is asleep, I sneak into his room and kiss his head. On that head is a scar. I kiss that scar and say thank you. Thank you for letting my baby be OK. There is divine timing for all of us—a time to be tested, a time to prove, a time to become.

That scar on MJ's head and the one above his left eye was because of me. We were in a car accident, and both sustained major injuries. Those were the darkest moments of my life, lying in the hospital bed awaiting surgery and also waiting for the prognosis of my child's head injury at a different hospital. For some miraculous reason, beyond the concussion and lacerations, he was fine. To this day, he talks about the accident, how everything went black and we went to sleep. He often says how lucky we are for a second chance. Sobering times can create doubt and faithlessness.

But that voice I heard telling me something bad was about to happen right before my car flipped and spun out of control proves to me that there is more at work, something behind the scenes. Accidents, illnesses, and death are inevitable; it isn't *if* they will happen but *when*. Near-death experiences change a person. It makes one evaluate their attachments to life and how they live.

In shamanistic cultures, shamans wear a human skull on their left shoulder to remind them how close they are to death each moment. The word *abhinivesa* means "leaning toward liking living." It is the strong ancestral impulse to want to be alive and carry the species forward. Negative entanglement occurs when one fears that something or someone might change. We must remember that everything is always in flux—the seasons, people—and if things are not growing, they are dying. Change is the only constant.

> "God is the name by which I designate all things which cross my willful path violently and recklessly."
> —Carl Jung

2.10. Subtle Afflictions Are to Be Minimized and Eradicated by the Process of Involution.

*Te pratiprasavaheyāh sūksmāh.*⁶¹*

The price is high; it will cost you your old life, your innocence, your identity. It will sever you from the world you once knew and everything familiar. You do not get to decide when or how. It comes unexpectedly and shakes up who you thought you were. Perhaps it is an addiction, a miscarriage, an accident, a sickness, a death, or a divorce. It's massive and destructive in nature, and it's like that purposely. It gets your attention. You feel weak and unprepared; you may crave what once was. The interim is the hardest part because you have not yet landed; you are in the void. The past looks inviting because at least it's something you know.

These initiations into the person you will become do not happen to you; they happen *for* you.

There are many small initiations in one's life—some so small you barely notice, others big and life-altering. An initiation is an act of sacrifice to the greater circle of life. An initiation is a rite of passage, an invitation to grow up.

Once you have experienced something that shakes you awake, you have the choice to heed the call or not. To heed the call requires copious amounts of courage. You have never navigated these lands, so you don't have the data or the mental circuitry yet. Imagination rules over experience. You go by feel. You listen to live, and you trust the pull of what you love.

> If you want what you've never had,
> you have to do what you've never done.
> How will you proceed?

You must consciously choose your thoughts (*pravritti*), stalk the afflictions, and trace them back to their roots. The more you know yourself, the more you know your patterns of running toward or away. To weaken or minimize the *kleshas* is to return to the source and remember you control your destiny. Yes, it hurts, and for a warrior to be brave, a warrior must be tender and sad. These tragic life events that change the trajectory of our lives are invitations for change and growth. It's about removing the shame and stigma around imperfect lives and actions. It's about sitting with those who feel unseen, unloved, uncomfortable. It requires maturity and selflessness.

This path of transformation requires a softening and compassion for yourself and what you have experienced. The old "dust your knees off" approach won't support this transition. It will require you to incubate, nourish yourself, and be taken care of. This stage often requires asking for help and taking the time to grieve.

Within each hardship, an opportunity is being gifted, the chance to go inward and metabolize the suffering and change our ways. If we are courageous enough to confront and overcome fear, we stay present, we stay clear. We control very little, and adversity reminds us of that. Injustice is often a catalyst for creation. Creation is the greatest act of generosity. To write, to sing, to paint, to move is consciously choosing where you put your energy. Your success teaches me nothing about you; your failures and responses to failures tell me everything.

> May our pain have not been in vain.

2.11. The Fluctuations of Consciousness Created by Gross and Subtle Afflictions Are to Be Silenced through Meditation.

Dhyānaheyāh tadvrttayah.[62]*

As though standing under a waterfall, the water represents our constant thinking. Meditation gives us the chance to step back to the rock ledge and watch the water, the thoughts, choosing which ones we want to think. Meditation is the act of giving one's full attention to only one thing as a way of becoming calm and relaxed. Through meditation, we observe the impulses of our minds (*vrittis*) in order to silence them and create a pause.

2.12. The Accumulated Imprints of Past Lives, Rooted in Afflictions, Will Be Experienced in Present and Future Lives.

Klesamūlah karmāsyah drsta adrsta janma vedanīyah.[63]*

Hindu mythology is interwoven through the postures of yoga. A myth is a powerful way to explain concepts that are difficult for the mind to grasp. In the third series of *ashtanga yoga*, we have *vasisthasana* (side plank), followed by *visvamitrasana* (fallen triangle). Strung through this sequence of postures is a story of karma and the playout of actions driven by greed and malice.

Visvamitra was a well-respected king with power, a bright future, and a passion for hunting. Vasistha was a great sage that lived in the forest perfecting meditation techniques and living in accordance with nonharm. On a hunting expedition, Visvamitra and his army came across Vasistha, who offered the king and his troops a meal. The meal came together in a matter of seconds and was extraordinary.

Visvamitra was floored by the exquisite meal and asked Vasistha how he had brought it together out of seemingly nowhere. Vasistha explained he had a magic cow, a gift from Indra, that provided him with anything he wished for. Visvamitra considered the usefulness of the cow and offered many tempting gifts in exchange, but Vasistha declined. In a fit of anger, Visvamitra took the cow by force. The cow, Nadindi, asked Vasistha what she had done wrong and why she was being given away. Vasistha explained he had not agreed to this exchange and that the cow could make her own decision.

Nandini was clear she did not want to be taken by force away from her master. In response to the aggression, Nadindi rose to her back legs, and out sprouted an army. Nandini's army destroyed Visvamitra's crew. Visvamitra was devastated and spiraled into a depression, realizing no amount of money or power could compare to spiritual prowess. Visvamitra wanted what Vasistha had: peace, nonviolence, and a magic cow. The king let go of his title and all his possessions to become a sage. He made many attempts to gain spiritual progress, but each time he gained momentum, he lost it because of his short temper. After many years and intense work, he gained control of his anger and was given the title of sage by Vasistha. Deep in his heart, he still held resentment toward Vasistha. This story articulates the impact of dark agendas and karma-inducing behaviors. Anything forced or fought for creates more karma and adds difficulty to one's ability in reaching presence.

All actions produce fruit. Actions driven by pain, anger, greed, and lust will give rise to other actions that are afflicted. Actions driven free from desire will lead to states of bliss. Through *kriya yoga* (*tapas*, *svadhyaya*, *isvarapranidhana*), we try to expunge in this life our residual karma that has gathered over past lives of this one.

2.13. As long as the Root of Actions Exists, It Will Give Rise to Class of Birth, Span of Life, and Experiences.

Sati mūle tadvipākah jati āyuh bhogāh.[64]*

Who are you when no one is watching? Do you act in accordance with societal norms, or are you true to your own heart? In the human realm of justice, we have courts, lawyers, juries, and judges to decide the verdict of one on trial. The cosmic justice system has us looking in the mirror at the one person we cannot lie to. Any actions motivated by a dark agenda will lead to more sorrow. We are creatures of action, so we must act, and in acting we must be aligned with our moral compass. Every action gives rise to a birth, a life span, and an experience. As yogis, we know that although sweet for a moment, addictive patterns run deep. Is the residue of the action worth it? Practice gives us a higher vantage point to look for our patterns. For the love of yourself, keep your heart sweet, and stay away from habits that hurt.

2.14. According to Our Good, Bad, or Mixed Actions, the Quality of Our Life, Its Span, and the Nature of Birth Are Experienced as Being Pleasant or Painful.

Te hlāda paritāpa phalāh punya apunya hetutvāt.[65]*

Actions drive the universe. Depending on the intentionality of our actions (good, bad, or mixed), the quality of our life is either a virtue or a liability. To live close to goodness is outlined in the eight-limb path in sutra 2.30.

2.15. The Wise Person Knows That Owing to the Fluctuations, the Qualities of Nature, and Subliminal Impressions, Even Pleasant Experience Are Tinged with Sorrow, and He Keeps Aloof from Them.

Parināma tāpa samskāra duhkaih gunavrtti virodhāt ca duhkham eva sarvam vivekinah.[66]*

The yogi knows that everything, even pleasant experiences, leads to pain. The conception of my child was out of love; the birth, great pain. I buy a home, I am elated. I pay my mortgage and money is tight, I worry. I practice, I'm strong and present. I injure my knee during practice, it hurts. And the world continues to turn. As the world turns, so do the qualities of nature, the *gunas*. In order to create anything, there is excitement (*rajas*), once created a sense of peace (*sattva*), and afterward a natural low (*tamas*). And one continues to play their role, understanding the purpose of their actions is to act without accumulating more karma. Everyone has a role to play, but the moment we get caught up in the "role," we lose the thread.

"There was once an old Chinese farmer
who had a horse to plough his fields.
One morning he woke up to discover the horse
had run away during the night.
Seeing this, his neighbor said,
'That's terrible. What are you going to do now?'
The farmer, who was a wise man, replied,
'Good news, bad news, who can say?'
A couple of days later, the horse returned,
accompanied by another horse.
This time, the neighbor said, 'What great good fortune!'
The farmer's response was the same:
'Good news, bad news, who knows?'
The farmer gave the second horse to his son, but soon
afterward, the horse threw him, and he broke his leg.
Seeing this, the neighbor said to the farmer,
'So sorry for the bad news about your son.
Who's going to help you on the farm now?'
To which the farmer answered,
'Good news, bad news, who can say?'
A week later, war broke out in the province. All the able-
bodied young men were drafted to fight.
Being injured, the farmer's son was spared.
The neighbor said, 'What a relief that
your son doesn't have to go to war.'
'Good news, bad news, who knows?' replied the farmer."
—Chinese parable

2.16. The Pains Which Are Yet to Come Can Be and Are to Be Avoided.

Heyam duhkham anāgatam.[67]*

As a coach, I am taught detached involvement. This means I care deeply about my client and am rooting for their highest good. I do not have an attachment to the result of their actions. Much like this concept, we attempt to act appropriately without strong attachments to the playout. Through a devoted yoga practice, we use techniques to break our physical boundaries and thus create stronger boundaries in our lives. In doing so, people, habits, and situations that don't serve begin to fall away. We begin to see where we have been porous with our self-care and sense of gratification. We develop a detached engagement with life—meaning, we are in this world, but not of it.

> If you keep your yoga up, you will be kept up.

We are not practicing because we are broken; we are practicing because we want to be free, free from drama, free from hooks, free to live our dharma.

2.17. The Cause of Pain Is the Association or Identification of the Seer (*Atma*) with the Seen (*Prakrit*), and the Remedy Lies in Their Dissociation.

Drastrdrsyayoh samyogah heyahetuh. [68]*

Squirrels hoard nuts. They hide them in random places, often forgetting where they put them. Bears, on the other hand, devour berries, twigs, and whatever they can sink their teeth into. A squirrel's wealth is about accumulation; a bear knows they are the wealth and therefore invests in themselves. Yogis, like bears, know they are the wealth, and by using their *sādhana* (practice of *hatha yoga*), they understand the material world, gain symbolic sight, and access *raja yoga*.

> "There can be no perfection if hatha yoga is without raja yoga or raja yoga without hatha yoga. Therefore, through practice of both, perfection is attained."
> —*Hatha Yoga Pradikipa* 2.76

Using the material world of success and failure, material possessions, and aging and dying as a reference for the soul is not deep enough. It is like hiding nuts, accumulating things. Pain happens when our soul (*atma*) identifies with what is being seen and *samyogah* occurs.

2.18. Nature Is Three Qualities (*Sattva, Rajas*, and *Tamas*), and Its Evolutes— the Elements (Mind, Senses of Perception, and Organs of Action)— Exist Eternally to Serve the Seer for Enjoyment of Emancipation.

Prakāsa kriyā sthiti sīlam bhūtendriyātmakam bhogāpavargārtham drsyam.[69]*

If we are using our lives to get to our High Self, we must actively participate in distinguishing between the material world (*prakriti*) and the universal consciousness (*purusa*). Using our yoga practices, we move from the biggest most obvious layer to the subtle. The material world consists of the *gunas* (*sattva, rajas, tamas*); the eleven *indriyas* (five senses, five organs of action, the mind); and the five *budtams* (water, earth, air, spirit, fire).

The *gunas* are the three qualities of everything material and can be afflicted or pure. According to cognitive behavior therapy, we have a thought, we act upon it, and afterward, we have a feeling about it. Action can be motivated by desire or judgment. Desire is based on passion, pull, and purpose. Judgment is self-critical and motivated by a "what's wrong with me?" attitude. The table below exhibits the two different ways I could have written this book. As the reader, you may not know the difference, yet as the author, they are radically different. This is an example of the *gunas* in operation.

	The Idea (Sattva)	The Execution (Rajas)	The Downtime (Tamas)
Positive	Stroke of insight to write the book—illumination	Actively writing and engaging with the material	Relaxation, nonaction
	Or	Or	Or
Negative	Striving to be good through effort, I write a book	Hustling with greed to create something worth reading	Being depleted, careless, a victim of my own laziness

When the *gunas* are virtuous, Pantanjali uses the words *prakasa*, *kriyā*, and *sthiti* for *sattva*, *rajas*, and *tamas*.

> "The person who is unperturbed amid praise or blame of himself, indifferent to honour and to disgrace, serene in success and failure, impartial to friend and foe, unattached to action that man has gone beyond the gunas."
> —*Bhagavad Gita* 14.25–26

The word *indriya* consists of two words: *in* ("subjects or objects of sense") and *dravanti* ("flow or moving toward"). The *indriyas* are the human senses or tools for gaining knowledge in our *sadhana*.

The eleven indriyas are the following:

- *Buddhi indriya*, the five senses that feed our mind with information about the exterior world: sight, hearing, taste, touch, and smell.
- *Karma indriya*, the five senses of actions that have us participate with the world: mouth for speech, hands for grasping, feet for walking, anus and rectum as organs of excretion, and genitals for organs of procreation.
- *Ubhaya indriya*, the manas—the basic, bureaucratic mind.

Using yoga techniques, we control and restrain the *indriyas* to find harmony and balance. To bring attention to our unconscious processes, we can uncover patterns that keep us stuck and find a way to enjoy life's pleasures and find freedom.

2.19. The *Gunas* Generate Their Characteristic Divisions and Energies in the Seer. Their Stages Are Distinguishable and Nondistinguishable, Differentiable and Nondifferentiable.

Visesa avisesa lingamātra alingāni gunaparvāni.[70]*

The polarity of what the outer world requires of you and how your own spirit directs you is the dance of life, our play, our *lila*. The secular world of family, friends, and fortune is on one side; the spiritual world of communion and commitment is on the other. The art of living a good life is learning to be in this world but not of it. The material world is cyclical, "birth, life, and death"; the *gunas* in flux. The *gunas* unfurl in an infinite number of ways, creating material. Through evolution, we become; through involution, we understand.

There are twenty-four is-nesses that make up the *gunas*, and they have four stages:

1. *Visesa*—particularized is made up of everything we see, hear, feel, taste, and touch, and it also allows us to interact with the external world: the five senses, five organs of action, and five elements. It also includes the thinking faculty of the mind, the *manas*.
2. *Avisesa*—unparticularized is made up of the five senses of actions that have us participate in the world (mouth for speech, hands for grasping, feet for walking, anus and rectum as organs of excretion, and genitals as organs of

procreation) and the higher function of the mind—the *ahamkara*, the I-maker.
3. *Linga*—cosmic intelligence is made up of the *buddhi*, which is our inner wisdom, our discernment, and our direct spiritual awareness, giving us the power to form and retain concepts, reasons, and comprehension.
4. *Alinga*—unmanifest is *mulaprakriti*, the root substance, that which exists in pure potential.

We experience the world from the most peripheral to the subtle *visesa* to *alinga*. And through *sadhana*, we work from the most subtle to the most obvious, *alinga* to *visesa*.

2.20. The Seer Is Pure Consciousness. It Witnesses Nature without Being Reliant on It.

Drastā drsimātrah suddhah api pratyayānupasyah.[71]*

What is the nature of the soul, and how does it differ from our intellect? Just as the wind gives the kite energy to explore the sky, the soul gives energy to a person to explore the world. The wind has no attachment to how high the kite flies, and neither does it die when the kite falls. Likewise, the soul has no attachment to a person's success or failure and does not die when the person exits the world. The soul (the *atma*) discerns between the material world and spirit. The intellect has a tendency to identify as the soul, and this is problematic because the intellect is made up of the manifest world, which is always changing through the phases of the *gunas*.

To still the body and mind is to access the intrinsic nature of the seer, which is wonder and presence (*svarūpe*). Once firmly established in the seat of one's soul, the yogi (as the kite can enjoy the power of the wind) can use the material form of the body and mind to participate in life.

"My ways and means are changing, 'cause I talk to spirit often.
Tell me to stay sharp, tell me to stay present.
Tell me to ignore the fools and focus on ascent.
Well, I said, 'I will starve my ego, and I will remain strong.
I will make mistakes and I will often be wrong.'
Well, I'm perfectly imperfect, and I'm only here to learn
And all the evil on the path gets burned."

—Satsang

2.21. Nature and Intelligence Exist Solely to Serve the Seer's True Purpose, Emancipation.

Tadarthah eva drsyasya ātmā.[72]*

An agent acts on behalf of another person. The agent seeks out opportunities and prepares the necessary arrangements to ensure the mission of the individual they represent is executed seamlessly. Our five senses and organs of action are the agents of our soul to execute its mission of seeing. The world entices our senses to engage with it and thus keeps us distracted. Through austere practice and a discerning mind, we learn to control our senses and our actions. Upon consciously choosing where to place their focus, the seer is free to do what it does—see. In order to see, there must be something to observe. Nature and all her wonders exist to free us from our suffering of distraction and identification. Everything is here to wake us up.

2.22. The Relationship with Nature Ceases for Emancipated Beings, Its Purpose Having Been Fulfilled, but Its Processes Continue to Affect Others.

Krtārtham prati nastam api anastam tadanya sādhāranatvāt.[73]*

There is no magic trick to becoming free from the material world. Our nature as human beings does not lend itself to devotion and nonattachment; therefore it is a path trudged through faithful work. Those fortunate enough to devote their lives to self-realization do so through consistent practice (*tapas*), the study of scripture (*svādhāya*), and devotion to God (*īsvarapranidhana*). Upon recognition that one is not their mind or body, they become free. This freedom allows one to participate in the world, offering their life up while residing in their truest nature (*svarūpe*). This is not the case for all beings. Many will spend their entire lives riding the roller coaster of aversion and attachment without an inkling that freedom is possible.

> "We are all just walking each other home."
> —Ram Dass

2.23. The Conjunction of the Seer with the Seen Is for the Seer to Discover His/Her/Their Own True Nature.

Sva svāmisaktyoh svarūpopalabdhi hetuh samyogah.[74]*

So much of our lives are spent reaching out for objects and others attempting to soothe and understand what is going on inside. We reach for relationships, work, material possessions, travel, creativity, and this is all part of the material world. Through yoga practice, we go inward for self-reflection, space, and spirit. The two worlds exist and merge for the seer to experience their true nature as witness and observer.

Our tendency to go outward has our intellect (*buddhi*) and sense of I-ness (*ahamkara*) believing that it is the seer. When this occurs, the mix-up continues. Over time we untangle from our identity and can see our High Self, our soul, reflected back at us, even when participating in the material world.

2.24. Lack of Spiritual Understanding (*Avidya*) Is the Cause of the False Identification of the Seer with the Seen.

Tasya hetuh avidyā.[75]*

The Volkswagen van, Mercedes Benz, Toyota RAV4, Tesla, and Honda Civic are all vehicles. Based on your lifestyle, upbringing, and socioeconomic class, you likely have a preference for one over the other. The vehicles are made differently to serve different purposes; the one similarity is that they transport people. This inanimate object does not have a consciousness to care if you like it more than one of the other vehicles. Unlike vehicles, we are conscious, and each of us is made differently to serve a different purpose. To compare oneself to a neighbor or a sibling is the root of suffering; it is ignorance (*avidyā*), and it is too small for you.

The cosmic game of dharma is to examine your life—the experiences you've had, your hardships, your preferences and aversions—and follow them back to the source, discovering where you are not free. We come into this world with a veil, a cloak, a forgetting. This veil (*maya*) keeps us separate and keeps the cosmic dance alive. Puncturing the veil allows us to step out of competition and judgment. Our hidden power lies in owning our individuality and, at the same time, our ordinariness. We share breath, we are connected, but nothing and no one compares to you.

2.25. The Destruction of Ignorance through Right Knowledge Breaks the Link Binding the Seer to the Seen. This Is *Kaivalya*, Emancipation.

Tad abhāvāt samyogābhāvah hānam taddrseh kaivalyam.[76*]

In captivity, baby elephants are tied to a tree by their ankle with a small rope. At first, the animal resists the rope and attempts to break free. After some time, the elephant accepts that it is only able to move the distance of the rope. As the elephant ages and grows in size and strength, the rope stays the same. Although fully capable of breaking the rope, the elephant accepts the parameters of the rope for the rest of its life. Much like the rope that binds the elephant to the tree, our minds bind us to life as we think we know it—accepting conditioning, our desires, learned helplessness, and our unhappiness as the way life is. Breaking free of our self-imposed binds releases us from other people's opinions and attachment to success and failure, which leads to a fully expressed life. Being fully expressed allows your personality to perform and the seer to watch with an aloof enjoyment. This contentment means there are no stakes in the deeds done, nor does your purpose depend on other people. The material world and its play exist for your enjoyment. The dance of life supports your skin in the game. If there was no game, there'd be no dance. Dance for the sake of dancing. Dance like no one's watching, or dance like at least someone is watching.

2.26. The Ceaseless Flow of Discriminative Knowledge in Thought, Word, and Deed Destroys Ignorance— the Source of Pain.

Vivekakhyātih aviplavā hānopāyah.[77]*

"Thank you for deciding to stay," the healer says through tears.

I'm numb.

My body feels broken beyond repair. The doctors say I won't handstand again. My child is severely concussed with shards of glass in his head, my spirit with my undriveable SUV in the impound lot.

"I wish I was dead," I whisper.

The nightmares of the car spinning and flipping. The lawyer calling to say the person who hit us has up to two years to sue me because I should have known about the black ice before my vehicle flipped and spun across two lanes of traffic to get hit head-on by this person's truck.

"It was your choice to stay, honey. Now you decide how to respond."

The aftermath of my accident is devastating. I grapple with the guilt of hurting my son and facing the uncertainty of income being self-employed and unable to work. Outside my experience, the world continues to spin. People get their groceries, host dinner parties, and laugh. I think to myself, "Will I laugh again?" People from my community come together to support me through this traumatic time. The love in my home is palpable with flowers, cards, meals, and my mother's presence.

The healer's words rattle around in my brain:

"Thank you for deciding to stay."

A *decision* is a "conclusion or resolution reached after consideration." Did I have a choice? When the world went black, did Micah and I have a round-table discussion, weighing the pros and cons of living versus dying?

I decide to believe this. Once healed, the world is different. My mother's eyes, greener. My child's skin, softer. Peaches, juicier. Laughter, more contagious.

A heightened sense of responsibility rises: to my child, my community, my world, my work. With my allegiance to servitude, the small stuff drops away. I see the power of my practice and that I am not my thoughts. Freedom, like the blue sky, is always there (*vivekakhyatih*), and the clouds of ignorance (*kleshas*) roll in to cover it. Our work, the play, is to remember how to become free. Using discriminative knowledge in our thoughts, words, and deeds destroys the roots of ignorance. The process of waking up cannot be undone.

2.27. Through This Unbroken Flow of Discrimination Awareness, One Gains Perfect Knowledge Which Has Seven Spheres.

Tasya saptadhā prāntabhūmih prajñā.[78]*

Matryoshka dolls, or Russian stacking dolls, are a set of wooden figures that separate at the middle and top from bottom to reveal a smaller figure of the same sort inside, which has, in turn, another figure inside it, and so on. Much like this, the yogis believe the human consists of seven layers: the outermost layer, your appearance; the innermost layer, your soul.

You present to the world with a certain eye color, height, and bone structure. These physical genetics were passed down through familial lines. This corporeal body is the *annamaya kosha*. Many people mistake this for the Self, using physical appearance and ableness as a reference for who you are, but that's not you.

Below aesthetics are the organs of sensing: taste, touch, smell, feel, and sight. The senses, although incredible, take us out and lead to attachment and aversion. One could easily mistake this for Self. But this is not you.

One layer below is our *pranic* body. This consists of the life force that animates your eyes, extends the lungs, and forces the blood to pulse blood through your veins. Through breath work and yoga, we intensify our connection to life and breath, the *pranyamaya kosha*. The edge between body and space blurs. One could remain here, calling this Self, but that is not you.

Below breath, we have our minds. The beautiful mind with its capacity to plan and execute, to judge and evaluate. This mind creates a reality with what it looks for and believes in; this is the *manomaya kosha*. Many get stuck here, believing they are their thoughts and fancy expressions, but this is not you.

In silent moments when the mind is still, one has access to higher intelligence. This part of you—untouched by the past, illusion, or the future—sees beyond form. The hint to call a friend at the exact moment they needed to hear your voice. *Vijñāna maya kosha*—"inner wisdom"—is a fine field to play in, but this is not you.

Below insight is an attentive consciousness. A place where nonperception of objects happens. This place, although still and wakeful, feels true enough to be you, and yet it is not.

At the center, the purest part of you sits, like the diamond with no flaws, purely reflecting everything. This place is self-illumined and beyond words. A deep knowing of what you are, where you came from, and what you fold back into (*ananda maya kosha*).

2.28. By Dedicated Practice of the Various Aspects of Yoga, Impurities Are Destroyed; the Crown of Wisdom Radiates in Glory.

Yogāngānusthānāt asuddhiksaye jñānadīptih āvivekakhyāteh.[79]*

The teacher is visiting from Montreal, Canada, and running a workshop at my home studio. I've been practicing for three years and feel proud of my progress. The morning session is a Mysore practice where fifty-year-olds are putting their legs behind their heads. To be honest, it makes me feel bad. I am comparing my tight hamstrings and belly fat to these gravity-defying angels. I feel jealous and competitive, and I want to be different than what I am. To distill it down beyond my insecurities, these yogis have something I want. They have purpose, grace, and devotion. It is clear we are all practicing, but for different reasons.

A beginner yogi is one who has practiced for less than ten years. This yogi is searching to belong and be seen. A beginner chases forms and determines a good or bad practice based on their performance and is hungry for change. The advanced student is devout. This practitioner has spent years studying their minds and strengthening their bodies. These yogis know it is not about the forms but rather showing up. Through devoted practice (*anusthanat*), the body and the mind of the yogi are purified. Unlike the beginner, who uses repetitive practice (*abhyāsa*) to gain freedom (*vairāgya*), the advanced yogi gains wisdom and achievement that is innocent and free of pride.

That moment, in that sweaty Mysore room, has catapulted me into the woman I am today. Through consistent practice, I've found a beauty I could not resist.

2.29. Morals (*Yamas*), Observations (*Niyama*), Posture (*Āsana*), Breath Work (*Prāṇāyāma*), Internalizing the Senses (*Pratyāhāra*), Concentration (*Dhāranā*), Meditation (*Dhyāna*), and Absorption (*Samādhi*) Are the Eight Constituents of Yoga.

Yama niyama āsana prāṇāyāma pratyāhāra dhāranā dhyāna samādhayah astau angāni.[80]*

Entrenched in the physical world, we are bound and blinded by our desires. We seek satiation in external things and get pulled by our likes and dislikes. By doing what we've always done, the spirit starves. We cling to our possessions hoping to soothe ourselves. The High Self whispers, "There is more for you." Through practice and discernment, we intervene by pulling apart the secular from the sacred. Like spokes on a wheel or steps on a ladder, the above sutra outlines the eight limbs of yoga. Each limb outlines the basics for living a morally aligned life.

2.30. Nonviolence, Truth, Abstention from Stealing, Chastity, and Absence of Greed for Possessions beyond One's Need Are the Five Pillars of *Yama*.

Ahimsā satya asteya brahmacarya aparigrahāh yamāh.[81]*

Yama is the Hindu god of death, the first person to have died and traveled the underworld. His experience allows him to guide souls in their mortality. Neither vengeful nor punishing, Yama is the judge of justice and the gatekeeper of the afterlife. Yama is exemplary of a yogi's choice to live for dying—the decision to align one's action with morality and go against the grain of our human conditions.

In the Ashtanga Opening Invocation, we address these human conditions as we chant the words, "*Samsara halahala mohashantyai.*" The direct translation is "relief from delusion and the poison of *samsara* (conditioned existence and memories)." This line speaks to the unconscious ways we repeat our suffering; by right action, we clear up our karma, knowing that each time we act, there is a counteraction.

The *yamas* in the context of the sutras are the first limb and refer to self-restraint in worldly matters. Acting on instinct will have us masking the truth, lashing out, taking what is not ours, having a heightened libido, or always wanting more. These innate human characteristics have us looking outside ourselves for salvation. By channeling this energy, we begin to build faith.

Wishing no harm to others; sincerity in word thought, action, and deed; integrity; chastity; and possessing only what one needs is a recipe for how to live in the secular world and be a yogi.

2.31. *Yamas* Are the Great, Mighty, Universal Vows Unconditioned by Place, Time, and Class.

Jāti desa kāla samaya anavacchinnāh sārvabhaumāh mahāvratam. [82]*

I'm lying in the bathtub after a big day of study, prayer, and practice. I hear a voice in my head say, "Wow, you are really starting to get this." And then I hear, "But do you really get it?" These teachings are so appealing to the ear and the ego. But what good is a quote if it does not inspire one to live better? The point of any mindful practice is freedom, freedom from our physical and emotional pain and freedom to be present. The dinner party talk with fancy Sanskrit is smoke and mirrors, distracting but not truly compelling. Let's keep our yoga alive and live the teachings. Instead of having a poster that says, "Be the change," let's be the change.

A *yama* is a great vow, a promise, an oath; to ask your own questions and find your own way. This requires honesty and self-evaluation. Each *yama* is a vow to the person you are becoming through the actions you take in relation to others. Regardless of religion, class, or country, these rules are universal and should be practiced unconditionally.

> "Dare to disagree."
> —David Whyte

2.32. Cleanliness, Contentment, Religious Zeal, Self-Study, and Surrender of the Self to the Supreme Self or God Are the *Niyamas*.

Sauca santosa tapah svādhyāya Īsvarapranidhānāni niyamāh.[83]*

> "How you gonna win if you ain't right within?"
> —Lauren Hill

To carry the torch, to be of service, means having your own back so that when called, you are ready. To be available in inconvenient moments is to be available. Disaster doesn't strike on our days off. What is in your self-care arsenal that prioritizes you? Do the foods you eat, company you keep, and habits you repeat give you energy and confidence? Are you moving forward or in circles?

How are you contributing to the world in a meaningful way?

Being of service is choosing transformation over transaction, and it is a philanthropic act. Transformation is about dropping one's ego in the name of connection and curiosity. It's about accessing another's heart, for no other reason than leaving the person a little better off than how you found them. Transactional is a "what is in it for me" attitude; it's shallow and short. It builds thick walls of judgment and separation. To be an agent of transformation requires deep conversations and piercing presence, but it does come at a cost: a disinterest in small talk.

The *niyamās* are how we build character; it's the work we do when no one is watching. Moving from the outermost layer (the physical body) to the subtle (our devotion). Cleanliness, contentment, fiery discipline, self-study, and surrender to God line us up with the High Self. We act with intent because we care deeply about our short time on the planet. The work on the mat is in preparation for life off the mat. Be sincere, be driven, be low-key.

2.33. Principles Which Run Contrary to *Yama* and *Niyama* Are to Be Countered with the Knowledge of Discrimination.

Vitarkabādhane pratipaksabhāvanam.[84]*

I used to practice yoga because I hated myself. I'd show up six days a week and destroy my body in the name of betterment. Injury was my badge of badassery. One day in Mysore, the teacher told me my legs were too short and shoulders too wide to do *dwipada sirsasana B* (both legs behind the head sitting upright). As the teacher moved on to the next tall, slim, gorgeous student, I sat and cried. I tucked my broken heart into my throat, closed my practice, and silently slipped away. After the rain comes the sun. Fighting my genetics is a losing battle and contrary to accepting what is (*santosha*). This teacher shone a light on the motivation behind my practice: my inadequacies. Now I practice clearing yesterday and opening myself to the mystery.

A practitioner must stalk the ways they act out of accordance with the *yamas* and the *niyamas*. When one discovers violence, dishonesty, stealing, sexual preoccupation, or greed, the suggestion is to go in the opposite direction (*pratipaksa bhavana*) and resist the great pull of such forces and take the opposing argument, yet toxic positivity doesn't work here. When the force of anger is alive, we must go deep into the root of the cause. To search for goodness is to go with the current and move toward the *niyamas* (*paksa bhavana*). Our practice is the outer expression of harmony within.

> "The best moments in our lives, are not the passive, receptive, relaxing times, although such experiences can also be enjoyable, if we have worked hard to attain them. The best moments usually occurred when a person's body or mind is stretched to its limits in a voluntary effort to

accomplish something difficult and worthwhile. Optimal
experience is thus something that we make happen. For
a child, it could be placing a trembling finger on the
last block on a tower she has built, higher than she has
built so far. For a swimmer, it could be trying to beat
his own record, for a violinist, mastering an intricate
musical passage. For each person there are thousands of
opportunities, challenges to expand ourselves."
—Mihaly Csikszentmihalyi

2.34. Uncertain Knowledge Giving Rise to Violence, whether Done Directly or Indirectly, or Condoned, Is Caused by Greed, Anger, or Delusion in Mild, Moderate, or Intense Degree. It Results in Endless Pain and Ignorance. Through Introspection Comes the End of Pain.

Vitarkah himsādayah krta kārita anumoditāh lobha krodha moha pūrvakah mrdu madhya adhimātrah duhkha ajñāna anantaphalāh iti pratipaksabhāvanam.[85]*

Himsa ("violence") can feel so righteous and powerful. You get cut off in traffic or passed over for a job you were best qualified for; you're furious, and it feels good. Yet anger begets anger and keeps you in turmoil. When faith is placed in the material world—that which we can see—we crave, seek pleasure, boost our ego, and want more. This insatiable appetite for things, fame, or people is our forgetting and keeps us small. You came here for a bigger reason, and although rationality and logic (*vitarka*) have their place, you must pan out to see the bigger picture. Is what you are doing getting you what you want? Each time you lash out, you lose power. Anger is from three sources, overindulgence in a sense of gratification taught or unconsciously induced. It can be mild, moderate, or intense.

To commit to the *yamas* and *niyamas*, one builds faith in what is not seen. Observation and self-reflection are the gateways to discovering the ways you continue to suffer. Bad things happen; what you do with that is up to you.

2.35. When Nonviolence in Speech, Thought, and Action Is Established, One's Aggressive Nature Is Relinquished, and Others Abandon Hostility in One's Presence.

Ahimsāpratisthāyām tatsannidhau vairatyāgah.[86]*

Belonging is quintessential to the human experience. When you feel understood, loved, and seen by the people around you—your friends, family, and community—you feel vibrant. The joy of being human is in our ability to relate and has us forming bonds with others at work, in sport, or online. Often, human connection occurs by sharing intimate details about other people lives. This tendency to gossip can lend itself to speaking ill of others behind their backs. The residue of speaking in a harmful way (*himsa*) leaves both participants on edge because it creates a space that is not safe. How then does one respond when the strong, familiar pull to connect through complaints about another arises?

Awareness of this culturally accepted way to commune gives space for a different response. If you would not share these details when the person you are talking about is present, it is not yours to share. An option would be to set a boundary by saying, "I don't feel comfortable talking about this," or suggesting that you bring the person in so the three of you can speak candidly. When you feel misunderstood or taken advantage of by another, this is an opportunity for honesty. Hard conversations can feel threatening, and yet they are the crossroads to a deepening of a relationship. When you remove gossip and rumination from your ways of connection, those around you will be compelled to do the same.

> "Great minds discuss ideas; average minds discuss events; small minds discuss people."
> —Eleanor Roosevelt

2.36. When the Practitioner Is Firmly Established in Truth, Their Words Become Potent That Whatever They Say Comes to Realization.

Satyapratisthāyām kriyāphalāsrayatvam.[87]*

The word *sincerely* comes from the Latin word *sin cera*, which translates as "without wax." In Rome, the base of pots was sealed with wax, and claims were made that they were watertight. In time the wax melted, rendering the pot useless for liquids. The meaning of "without wax" is authenticity and without gimmicks. How often do we embellish the details, brush over the truth, or diminish our words in order to protect another or the self? Fear of judgment and hard conversations linger in the stage wings of our consciousness. The cost of being dishonest is fraudulence, shallow relationships, and people-pleasing. The second *yama*—*satya* ("truthfulness")—is a vow to use your words with care and accept all parts of yourself. Once established in a practice of truth, your power is undeniable. You are someone others can trust.

> "I want to know if you can disappoint
> another to be true to yourself.
> If you can bear the accusation of
> betrayal and not betray your own soul."
> —Oriah Mountain Dream

A great king wanted to protect the kingdom by building a brick wall around it. The king hired the greatest stonemasons. After the job was completed, the king and the king's heir did an inspection. The king noticed one brick slightly broken. He said, "We must fix this." To which the heir replied, "No one will notice." The king said, "If we get attacked and the kingdom falls because of that weakness, both you and I will know." It takes real courage to face your own conscience and question your own integrity. You are responsible for your character and must repair your spirit when it is out of alignment. We can lie to ourselves for a little while, but eventually, we bump up against our truth.

> "Truth is beauty, beauty is truth."
> —John Keats

2.37. When Abstention from Stealing Is Firmly Established, Precious Jewels Come.

Asteyapratisthāyām sarvaratnopasthānam.[88]*

The cashier forgets to charge you for the apples. You take a pen from your workplace. You repeat something profound you heard somewhere else and claim the words as your own. The meeting is at one o'clock, but you show up at one fifteen.

It's insidious; it slips between the cracks. It feels morally okay because it isn't blatant stealing if it is unintentional. A sense of abundance rushes in; you've won, gained something without having to pay. In truth, there is always a fee—that fee, your authenticity. Get intimate with this *yama*: *asteya* ("nonstealing of time, attention, and resources"). Observe the casual ways you take what is not rightfully yours. When one refrains from stealing, everything is provided.

2.38. When the Practitioner Is Firmly Established in Abstinence, Knowledge, Vigor, Valor, and Energy Flow to Him.
Brahmacaryaprastisthāyām vīryalābhah. [89]*

Had I known it would be the last time, I would have savored it, been gentler, lingered longer. The taste of my grandmother's oatmeal cookies, the sound of Clara's laugh, the nape of my lover's neck. Occasions come and gone, precious moments I missed because I was in a hurry to get to the next moment.

Brahmacarya, the fourth *yama*, loosely translates as "refraining from sexual preoccupation," yet its essence is the art of moderation. To be moderate is to have discipline around the sense of gratification and to enjoy the moment. Controlling and directing the senses is choosing where you put your efforts and energy. Sexuality and overindulgence are energy leaks and lead to wanting more. Enjoy the luxuries of living, but ensure you control them instead of them controlling you. Addiction is described as something that almost works. Take your time with the beautiful things. Imagine it was your first and last time.

2.39. Knowledge of Past and Future Lives Unfolds When One Is Free from Greed for Possessions.

Aparigrahasthairye janmakathamtā sambodhah.[90]*

Fists clenched, we cling, become dependent on accumulation, defined by what we own. This want for wealth or power is often driven by a need for validation.

Aparigraha, the final *yama*, translates as "nonhoarding or without greed." To be ambitious is admirable, and we must stay close to the pulse of why we do what we do. To release our grip on fame and fortune frees us from a competitive mindset. To open oneself to the collective good—be it your staff, your clients, your product—allows energy to flow and everything you want to follow. The oyster does not own the pearl it makes, but the oyster's inner landscape is shaped by that pearl.

> "The things we own, end up owning us."
> —*Fight Club*

2.40. Cleanliness of Body and Mind Develops Disinterest in Contact with Others for Self-Gratification.

Saucāt svāngajugupsā paraih asamsargah.[91]*

To be disliked is my Achilles' heel. I used to overextend and overfunction to prove I was worthy. Give to get, be to have. That's an old program. I don't buy likes anymore.

When I dislike another, it reveals jealousy and anger within me. When I feel its frenetic pull, I ask the mother / the guru / God to take it from me. When I am disliked, I no longer feel the need to fix it; just an awareness of how heavy the need to be liked weighs on me. It's not about not being liked; rather, the cost of carrying victimization in my heart, that's hatred. Hatred does not dispel hatred; love does.

Saucā, the first *niyama*, is the positive action one takes to clean up the physical body, the internal body, and the emotional body. With this ownership of self, confidence is gained, and the external eye becomes less important.

2.41. When the Body Is Cleansed, the Mind Purified, and the Senses Controlled, Joyful Awareness Needed to Realize the Inner Self Also Comes.

Sattvasuddhi saumanasya aikāgrya indriyajaya ātmadarsana yogyatvāni ca.[92]*

The yoga practice is designed to purify the practitioner, from the external to the internal. It starts with the promise of youth and shiny eyes. We see the results almost instantly: we get strong and fit. The next stage is a little more esoteric: to cleanse our energetic bodies. This is done through breath work (*pranayama*) and physical locks (*mudras*) in the body. We breathe deeper, and we feel more alive in our skin. The last stage, the most beautiful one, is the purification of the mind. This happens when for a brief moment, we forget our pain and suffering. We are no longer driven by our addictions, our fears, or our hate. When the mind functions in this, we act skillfully and karmas are dissolved. This cleansing (*sauca*) transcends the mat and meditation cushion as we become aware of all the details around us. A sense of peace arises, knowing we are taking care of what is in our hands to take care of.

2.42. From Contentment and Benevolence of Consciousness Comes Supreme Happiness.

Santosāt anuttamah sukhalābhah. [93]*

To my right, I watched a house burn: firefighters working to tame the flames while residents are crying as they stare in horror. To my left I watched children laughing and playing, full of life. How exemplary this scene is of life. The suffering, the joy, and the dichotomy of it all. It reminds me of my favorite teachers, great teaching: nothing is ever one thing. The mind loves to globalize. The house is burning; it's the worst. The children are joyful; it's the best. Everything is nuanced, layered, and symbolic. Yoga's biggest intention is to create space for mystery. Yoga teaches us to be content. Contentment is being neither *for* nor *against*; it is not apathy or indifference but a warm engagement with the world without being troubled by it. With contentment (*santosa*), your aim is to remain disenchanted, free of the spell that is cast by pleasure and pain. This way you are neither disappointed nor dissatisfied with life. Almost nothing can knock you off your center.

> "Out beyond ideas of wrongdoing and rightdoing,
> there is a field. I'll meet you there."
>
> —Rumi

2.43. Self-Discipline (*Tapas*) Burns Away Impurities and Kindles the Sparks of Divinity.

Kāya indriya siddhih asuddhiksayāt tapasah. [94]*

How badly do you want it?

Like the pressure, heat, and time required to turn coal into diamonds—the enthusiastic, fierce discipline of a practitioner turns doubt into engagement and separation into love. *Tapas* is the momentum created through honest practice. Teaching our scattered minds to dwell on one spot—be it our big toe in triangle pose or the bottom of our exhale—is our resolute decision to be present. Yoga is our discipline to help strengthen our spirit. The purification happens as we hit the Reset button each time we get on our mats, leaving the past in the past and the future in the future, to land right here and now. The yogi knows: no perfect beach, financial success, or deep backbend will fill the void in our hearts. The body is our rental car, and any attachment to or obsession with the vehicle will lead you to suffer. Take care of your body because you love its functions, and use it to access the present moment. Much like the durability of a diamond because of its formation process, *tapas* (commitment to practice) is our stability, staying power, and a direct line to living our dharma.

2.44. Self-Study Leads toward Realization of God or Communion with One's Desired Deity.

Svādhyāyāt istadevatā samprayogah.[95]*

Intimacy is a close, familiar bond or relationship. Intimacy is not a fleeting love affair, nor is it reserved for those with whom you share a physical relationship. Intimacy is about longevity and safety. It develops over time and is the exploration of closeness through the highs and the lows of our humanity. External relationships are a great place to start, to watch our patterns of running and chasing. However, our longest, most important relationship is with ourselves, so we ought to study it (*svādhāya*). To look closely at this relationship, we must consider where we let ourselves down, put too much pressure on ourselves, and didn't listen to our intuition. The word *drishti* ("gazing point") comes from the word *drashtu* ("watcher, seer, witness"). *Drashtu* is an unconditionally loving presence that watches over. Scripture and myths aid one in understanding this all-loving, all-powerful energy. To merge the seer with the seen is to see oneself through that tender lens. When you are well loved, well slept, and well fed, this concept is easy, but this sutra speaks to the hard days of self-loathing and confusion. We come into this world alone, and we die alone. The only person we answer to is ourselves.

2.45. Surrender to God Brings Perfection in *Samadhi*.
Samādhisiddhih Īsvarapranidhānāt.[96]*

By going myopic and studying our bodies through *sādhana* ("practice"), we learn that we are not our bodies, and therein lies freedom. Becoming flexible and fluid kinesthetically prepares the body for the big work of becoming nobody and entering the present moment. Removing our conditioned ways of clinging to a fixed identity, we open to the unknown (*īsvara*). By going beyond self and our 3-D realities, we experience pure consciousness (*samādhi*). This state of possibility and inspiration is the birthplace of our truest intention. Surrendering our fears and expectations, we trust and harness the energy of that which cannot be seen.

2.46. Asana Is Perfect Firmness of Body, Steadiness of Intelligence, and Benevolence of Spirit.
Sthira sukham āsanam.[97]*

Buddhists talk about a beginner's mind: an attitude of openness, eagerness, without preconceived notions. Having a beginner's mind when you are a beginner is easy, but what about after years of experience? Can you remain curious?

In *yogasana*, we are looking for the immovable spot where effort and ease meet. This is done through an anchor point downward (hands or feet) and using that point to reach upward. It's about creating space in the physical body and our minds. *Sthira* translates as "steady, fixed, dependable" and is our boundaries in the posture. *Sukha* is "spacious, sweet, soft" and is our finesse. The precarious ratio of *sthira* to *sukha* shifts day to day, posture to posture. Too much *sthira* leads to aggression, and too much *sukha* leads to boredom. Each time you step on the mat, you are given a choice: to evolve or remain. If you remain the same, everything repeats: the same storms, the same lessons. Use your practice to explore what lies outside your comfort zone.

2.47. Perfection in Asana Is Achieved When the Effort to Perform It Becomes Effortless and the Infinite Being Within Is Reached.

Prayatna saithilya ananta samāpattibhyām.[98]*

To be impeccable is to be in accordance with one's highest standard. Impeccable is not perfection, as perfection indicates one standard that everyone must meet. The practice is individual as body types and concentration differ among practitioners. Knowing oneself is understanding where and when to place more or less effort to access the immovable spot. Perseverance when applied to the forms, the gazing point, and the breath trains the mind to unite with the body and spirit, to access wholeness (*samāpatti*). Impeccable is from the Latin words *in* ("not") and *peccare* ("to sin"). Being without sin is to remove the human stuff—the shame, the desire, the greed—and enter the infinite energy of your life, your masterpiece. Be in your own energy, and stop diluting yourself; there is more for you.

> "I am chin up, best foot forward, stick my landings."
> —Buddy Wakefield

2.48. From Then On, the *Sādhaka* Is Undisturbed by Dualities.

Tatah dvandāh anabhighātah.[99]*

When the polarity of pleasure and pain, desire and aversion, no longer grips the attention, the mind field stops. This state, unaffected by opposites, is when the body, mind, and soul are in the same place at the same time. Using pairs of opposites—right/left, up/down—we land in the generous present moment.

2.49. *Pranayama* Is the Regulation of the Incoming and Outgoing Flow of Breath with Retention. It Is to Be Practiced after Perfection in Asana Is Attained.

Tasmin satisvāsa prasvāsayoh gativicchedah prānāyāmah.[100]*

Our breath is our connection to life, and yet we rarely explore it. Left unattended, it is irregular and unconscious. The fourth limb is *pranayama*. It consists of two words: *prana* ("life force") and *ayamah* ("extension"). Breath work is advised only after one has gained proficiency in physical yoga. This stipulation indicates the power of breath work and the necessity to prepare the physical container. *Prana* does not refer only to breath; it is our mind, spirit, sexuality, and power. The literal components of breath are threefold: an inhalation (wherein we draw oxygen in through the nose or mouth, creating space in the body), an exhalation (wherein we expel oxygen out of the nose or mouth, creating a contraction in the body); and the retention, or control, at the top or the bottom of the breath.

2.50. *Pranayama* Has Three Movements: Prolonged and Fine Inhalation, Exhalation, and Retention—All Regulated with Precision According to Duration and Place.

Bāhya ābhyantara stambha vrttih desa kāla samkhyābhih paridrstah dīrgha sūksmah.[101]*

How do we make our breath practice as captivating as our physical yoga practice?

Breath has three components: the physical location (*desa*), length (*kala*), and precision (*samkhyabhih*).

The locations of the five *vayus* ("wind, air") are the following:

- *Prana vayu*—diaphragm and collar forward-moving air—is the energizing force of vital energy moving inward: respiration, ideas, forward motion.
- *Apana vayu*—navel and pelvis air that moves away—is the outward and downward movement of energy associated with elimination.
- *Samana vayu*—pelvis, assimilations, the balancing air, inner absorption, digestion.
- *Udana vayu*—throat and upper palette—that which carries upward, speech, expression, breath, and eating.
- *Vyanu vayu*—chest—integrates all other vayus, circulation, and expansion.

The correlation between breath movement and mind activity (*vrittis*) is where things get interesting. An inhalation draws the focus inward, and the possibility of thought is high. An exhalation draws the focus outward, to listening and emptiness. The retention at the top of the inhale feels exciting, and the retention on the exhale is the closest to death we will experience while being alive.

Like a set of Russian stacking dolls, in which wooden dolls of decreasing size are placed one inside another, the human is made up of five layers: the physical body, breath body, mind body, intuition body, and bliss body (*annamaya, pranamaya, manomaya, vijnanamaya, anandamaya kosha*). During an inhalation, one moves from the bliss body to the physical body, from consciousness (*purusa*) to self (*prakriti*). During an exhalation, one moves from the physical body to the bliss body, from self (*prakriti*) to consciousness (*purusa*).

To seal ourselves off from the external world and study the breath is to see that inside each of us is the entire universe.

2.51. The Fourth Type of *Pranayama* Transcends the External and Internal *Pranayamas* and Appears Effortless and Nondeliberate.

Bāhya ābhyantara visaya āksepī caturthah.[102]*

What was laborious turns automatic through repetition and practice. We learn to lift our arches in standing work, and that carries through to the seated work without actively working our feet. This element of alignment in asana allows the life force to flow and a state of concentration to be reached on the mat. The fourth element of *pranayama* is in the embodiment of it without conscious effort. After years of practice and study, our *pranayama* becomes effortless, bringing the doer and the doing together, and the union of the body, mind, and spirit happens.

2.52. *Pranayama* Removes the Veil Covering the Light of Knowledge and Heralds the Dawn of Wisdom.

Tatah ksīyate prakāsa āvarnamam.[103]*

I'm giving a yoga talk. I'm in the flow, a channel, preparedness meeting opportunity, when suddenly I lose it, I slip back into the identity of "teacher."

Do they like this? Am I making sense?

I'm out of presence and in *avidyā* ("nonseeing, ignorance"). I've fallen for my own carnival show. It's like this for all of us. A merry-go-round of waking up and falling back asleep. My trip—teacher/teachings/student. Your trip is something different but similar. We all have parts to play; our only job is to use our gifts to burn karma and get to presence. When the perceiver, the object of perception, and the process of perception merge, that is presence—that is what we are after. *Pranayama* allows us to pierce our illusion of separateness from source and removes the *kleshas* ("veils") that prevent us from seeing.

2.53. The Mind Becomes Fit for Concentration.

Dhāranāsu ca yogyatā manasah.[104]*

A lifetime of habituation has us trapped in distraction, reaching for our phones, computers, other people. This constant state of arousal has us addicted to chaos, mistaking the material world for our purpose. Taking a step back and going against the grain is harnessing one's true power of attention. A scattered mind is powerless; a focused mind has limitless potential.

Yogyatā ("fitness") for concentration is built through physical yoga, breath work, and *mudras*. Start small with something you love. *Dhāranā* ("concentration") is a byproduct of doing what you love. It is the ability to focus so intently that the world around you stands still. The focus could be physical (tree pose), internal (meditation), an object (candle), or a sound (*aum*). It is the timeless place where the mind is absorbed and fully transfixed. Pouring oneself into the moment requires preparation and maturity. The insight that you are powerless and distracted is useless unless you act. Each small act to stay present is flexing the muscle of *dhāranā*.

2.54. Withdrawing the Senses, Mind, and Consciousness from Contact with External Objects and Then Drawing Them Inward toward the Seer Is *Pratyahara*.

Svavisaya asamprayoge cittasya svarūpānukārah iva indriyānām pratyāhārah.[105]*

What a luxury to engage with the splendors of the world through our five senses. These worldly pleasures have a profound pull and with that the ensnarement of desiring more. Allowing the five senses to chase the objects of their desire is outsourcing your agency to the external world, and that is dangerous. Marketers prey on your senses going outward; they stalk your insecurities and provide products that will surely eradicate your suffering. The onus is on you to reclaim your attention and remember your brilliance (*svaūpe*).

Like the reigns of the chariot driver directing the horses, *pratyāhāra* is to pull back on the senses and turn them inward. In *yogasana*, we choose one spot to place our eyes, a *drishti*. This gazing point is the resolute decision not to look anywhere else. In controlling the sense of sight, we create a lock, an energetic seal, closing the posture and keeping the power inside.

The power is in choosing when to reach out and when to retreat.

2.55. *Pratyahara* Results in the Absolute Control of the Sense Organs.

Tatah paramā vasyatā indriyānām.[106]*

The colors of a sunset, new love, laughter, and a broken heart sound the alarm bells of coasting and stop us dead in our tracks. With a sudden break in the pattern, the opportunity to see with unclouded eyes arises. Yet day to day, how many practices do we have that bring us directly into the present moment? As we rush to meet deadlines, get groceries, finish the dishes, most of us are operating on autopilot. We make our morning coffee out of habit, already thinking of how it will aid us in our productivity. This known nature of going through our days in a daze is *samskāra*. The easiest path with the least resistance is a glorified groove, which is actually a rut. *Samskāras* have us repeating our pasts and calling it a future. The necessity of something to shake us from our mindlessness into spontaneity is why we practice yoga.

To master the senses is to luxuriate in them—savoring, reveling, basking, and appreciating how and when we choose to participate in the world. Power is the choice to engage with our senses or reclaim them (*pratyāhāra*). Take back your day, and add ceremony into as much as you can. Truly listen, taste, smell, feel, and see what is right in front of you.

Conclusion

At the end of yoga practice, we bring our hands together in prayer and take our thumbs to our sternum in *anjali mudra*. This *mudra* represents the teacher-student bond: one hand (the student) yearns for understanding, and the other hand (the teacher), has both passion and experience for the subject. The two come together and reach for the light to break the bonds from the past and the mix-up that we are the material body. The teacher could not exist without the student and vice versa; they need each other

To my readers, all my insights through practice and contemplation are in honor of our awakening and our promise to keep the lineage of yoga alive. Without you, none of this would be possible.

Thank you for working hard to understand the perplexing 1 percent of yoga that is the philosophy behind it. I urge you to revisit these sutras. When you feel pain, use one of the sutras as a lens to study your discomfort. To truly understand these teachings, we must embody and integrate them.

As Heraclitus said, "No man ever steps in the same river twice. For it's not the same river and he's not the same man." As you continue to evolve and mature, the sutras will hold different meanings.

Go forth, my loves, and conquer.
Believe in your daydreams, and follow your passion.
You matter.
This is just the beginning.
Yoga happens now!

Roots of the Yoga Sutras

A tapestry is woven by hand or loom and is said to contain the artist's ancestry and life's work. The artist knows the final image they wish to create and therefore works backward, reverse engineering their vision. The yoga sutras speak to our shared humanity and how to transcend the mental concepts that keep us separate. *Sutra* translates as "thread"; therefore, the yoga sutras are written as a tapestry that holds the gamut of yoga together, leading us to the final stage which is union with one's High Self. Patanjali, the author, is said to be a sage from the second century before the Christian era.

Patanjali was a Sanskrit scholar and worked intensively on Ayurvedic medicine. The sutras written two thousand years ago are Patanjali's life work and a blend of the Samkhya school of Indian thought, Buddhism, and Jainism. Traditionally, the sutras were passed on orally through chanting. Students were to learn the sutras forward and backward. These teachings were kept a secret on purpose because of their power.

Now more than ever, we need these teachings. In written form, the sutras are a book of 195 aphorisms, or *sutras* ("threads"), which are words of wisdom on the path of yoga. This text is split into four *pādas* (translated as "feet" or "chapters"—and is written in Sanskrit. *Sanskrit* (not *Sanskript*) translates as "polished, or perfect." Think of Sanskrit as a "trim-the-fat diet," where only the nutritious remains. What would take an entire paragraph in English to articulate takes only a few words in Sanskrit.

As Sanskrit is not our mother tongue, we have no past reference to the words, and our minds cannot attach a story or meaning. This inability to quickly interpret the words on autopilot allows for curiosity to integrate and understand the words and their meaning in this context.

- *Samkhya School*

The Samkhya school is an orthodox school of Indian thought. This dualistic system suggests there are two realities at work: the *prakrti*, which translates as "nature or condition" (individual mind), and the *purusa*, which translates as "consciousness." *Prakriti* is everything in the material world that is impermanent and always in flux (birth, life, death cycle). The three qualities of the material world are the *gunas*. The three *gunas* are *rajas* ("activity, productivity"); *tamas* ("lethargy, slow movement"); and *sattva* ("purity and equanimity").

Our yoga practice attempts to liberate us from seeing the world through the changing material world (*prakrti*) and to observe the essence of existence, which is ever present and never changing (*purusa*).

- *Buddhism*

Unlike the Samkhya school, the Buddhists believe that anyone can experience the "truth" or become enlightened. You need not come from a specific caste nor be a certain gender to become enlightened. Another piece of Buddhism we find in the yoga sutras is in sutra 1.33, the *brahmaviharas*—the four virtues or qualities of the heart.

- *Mahavir Jain*

Saint Mahavir Jain developed Jainism. Jainism is a religion that believes freedom and enlightenment are gained only when one lives in a nonharmful way (*ahimsa*). After spending much time in silence and meditation, Saint Mahavir Jain realized that the three jewels for living a spiritual life are right belief, right knowledge, and right conduct.

The one addition Pantanjali made to the melding of these three philosophies is *īsvara*. *Īsvara* is the Sanskrit word for "the divine." He left this open-ended with no particular name, and in doing so, the practice becomes available to anyone no matter their religious bend. Yoga is a devotional practice—each asana a *mudra* ("seal"), each breath a *mantra* ("prayer"). To devote your practice to something more powerful than you allows you to progress along the path of yoga more quickly.

When we attribute our success to something other than ourselves, it becomes a surrender to grace. The ego steps out of the way, and we nourish our connection to the divine and everyone around us. The information is magical and, when applied, will change the way you see the world and yourself.

About Erin Evans

Erin Evans has studied, taught, and practiced yoga for over twenty years. She is fascinated by human behavior and committed to guiding others to find joy and purpose in their lives. Erin has written and led 200- and 300-hour Yoga Teacher Trainings around the world. Her affinity for Sanskrit, sense of humor, and devotion to the practice make the ancient teachings relevant to her readers.

A modern yogi, a mother, an entrepreneur, a podcaster, and a mindset coach, Erin is always in the seat of the student. Armed with a business degree, a 500-hour Yoga Teacher Training, and a professional coaching program, Erin's work is to aid people to make the impossible possible and find freedom.

About *Unraveled*

This book is a compendium for the modern yogi. It uses personal stories and anecdotes to unravel the first two *pādas* of the *Yoga Sutras of Patanjali*.

To practice yoga is to engage with life, and insight without application is useless; therefore, yoga without integration is just gymnastics.

Beyond the stylish yoga gear, the motivational quotes, and the sweaty forms, there is a vast ocean of teachings on how to navigate the richness of life. This approach to the yoga sutras has never been done. This tongue-in-cheek, reverent, and humorous take on a serious topic is insightful and heartwarming. The narrative brings the content to life, showing us how to live these principles off the mat.

Glossary

1* *atha*—now, auspicious, a prayer
yoga—union; to yoke the body, mind, and spirit
anusasanam—advice, instructions, order

2* *yogah*—union, integration from outermost layer to innermost self
citta—mind, the vehicle of observation and attention
vrtti—movements of thought, waves of rumination and contemplation
nirodhah—still point, stopping, directing, refraining

3* *tada*—then
drastuh—the seer, the soul
svarupe—in their own
avasthanam—rests, dwells, resides, radiates

4* *vrtti*—fluctuations, behaviors, busy mind
sarupyam—closeness, identification
itaratra—at other times, elsewhere

5* *vrttayah*—movement, modification
pancatayyah—fivefold
klista—afflicted, tormented, painful
aklistah—untroubling, pleasing, undisturbing

6* *pramana*—correct knowledge
viparyaya—contrary, inverted
vikalpa—doubt, indecision, hesitation, fantasy
nidra—sleep
smrtayah—memory

7* *pratyaksa*—direct perception
anumana—inference
agamah—traditional texts, a person whose word we can rely on
pramanani—kinds of proof

8* *viparyayah*—unreal
mithyajnanam—illusory knowledge
atadrupa—not in its own form
pratistham—occupying, standing, seeing

9* *sabdajnana*—verbal knowledge
anupati—followed in sequence, pursued
vastusunyah—devoid of things and meaning
vikalpah—imagination and fantasy

10* *abhava*—nonexistence
pratyaya—going toward, trust, confidence, instrument, understanding
alambana—support, abode
vrttih—thought wave
nidra—sleep

11* *anubhuta*—perceived
visaya—an object, an affair, a transaction
asampramosah—slip away
smrtih—memory

12* *abhyasa*—repeated practice
vairagyabhyam—freedom from desires, detachment
tannirodhah—restrain

13* *tatra*—of these, in that case
sthitau—as regards steadiness
yatnah—continuous effort
abhyasah—practice

14* *sa*—this
tu—and
dirghakala—for a long time
nairantarya—without interruption

satkara—dedication, devotion, truth-making
asevitah—zealously, practiced
drhhabhumih—a firm ground, rooted

15* *drsta*—perceptible, visible
anusravika—heart, oral testimonial
visaya—object
vitrsnasya—freedom from desire, contentment
vasikara—bringing under control
samjna—consciousness, intellect
vairagyam—detachment, indifference to the world, renunciation

16* *tatparam*—highest, most excellent, the purest
purusakhyateh—the highest knowledge of the soul
gunavaitrsnyam—indifference to the qualities of nature: inertia
(*tamas*), passion (*rajas*), and serenity (*sattva*)

17* *vitarka*—analytical thinking, argument, inference
vicara—reason, meditation, insight
ananda—bliss, felicity
asmitarupa—consciousness of being one with self
anugamat—grasping, following, comprehending
samprajnatah—distinguish, know actually

18* *virama*—rest, pause
pratyaya—conviction, confidence, going toward
abhyasa—practice
purvah—before, old, previous
samskaraesah—balance of subliminal impressions
anyah—other, different

19* *bhava*—true condition, real disposition
pratyayah—going inward
videha—without material existence
prakrtilayanam—merge in nature

20* *sraddha*—trust, faith
virya—strength, energy, power
smrti—memory

samadhi—profound meditation, devotion
prajna—awareness of real knowledge acquired through contemplation
purvakah—previous, prior
itaresam—another, rest, different

21* *tivra*—intense, sharp, poignant
samveganam—cheerful, quick
asannah—near in time, approached

22* *mrdu*—soft, mild
madhya—middle, average
adhimatratvat—ardent, steady, keen
tatah—further, thence
api—also
visesah—differentiation

23* *isvara*—the Lord, Universal Soul
pranidhanat—contemplation, prayer, renunciation
va—or

24* *klesa*—affliction, pain
karma—act, perform
vipaka—seat, abode
asyaih—untouched
aparamrstah—unaffected, in no way connected
purusaviesah—a special person
isvarah—God

25* *tatra*—in him
niratisayam—matchless, unrivaled
sarvajna—all-knowing, omniscient
bijam—a seed, origin, beginning

26* *sa*—that
esah—*purusa*, god
purvesam—first, foremost
api—also, too
guruh—master
kalena—time
anavacchedat—unbounded, continuous

27* *tasya*—him
vacakah—signifying, indicating
pranavah—the sacred sound of aum

28* *tat*—that
japah—muttering, whispering, repeating
tadarthabhavanam—its aim and purpose, its meaning and feeling

29* *tatah*—then
pratyakcetana—individual soul
adhigamah—to find, discover, accomplish
api—also
antaraya—intervention, interference, obstacle
abhavah—absence
ca—and

30* *vyadhi*—disease
styana—lack of interest, sluggishness
samsaya—doubt, indecision
pramada—carelessness, negligence
alasya—physical laziness
avirati—lack of moderation
bhrantidarsana—living under illusion
alabdhabhumikatva—missing the point, inability to hold on to what is achieved
anavasthitatvani—unsettled, inability to maintain progress
cittaviksepah—scattered, oscillating mind
te—these
antarayah—obstacles, impediments

31* *duhkha*—sorrow, pain, unhappiness
daurmanasya—mental pain, affliction, despair
angamejayatva—unsteadiness of the body
svasaprasvasah—inspiration and expiration
viksepa—scattered, distracted
sahabhuvah—side by side

32* *tatpratisedhartham*—for their prevention
eka—one

tattva—a real state, truth, a principle, a doctrine
abhyasha—practice

33* *maitri*—friendliness
karuna—compassion
mudita—gladness, joy
upeksanam—indifference
sukha—happiness
duhkha—sorrow
punya—virtue
apunya—vice
visayanam regarding an object, concerning a thing
bhavanatah—conception, object
cittaprasadanam—graceful diffusion of the consciousness, a favorable disposition

34* *pracchardana*—emitting, sending forth
vidharanabhyam—restraining, supporting
va—or, an option
pranasya—of breath

35* *visayavati*—related, attached to
va—or
pravrttih—onward, advancing, progressing, devoting
utpanna—born, accomplished
manasah—mind
sthiti—state
nibandhani—origin, foundation

36* *visoka*—free from grief, sorrowless
va—or
jyotismati—luminous, shining, tranquil

37* *vita*—devoid
raja—passion
visayam—object
va—or
cittam—consciousness

38* *svapna*—dream
nidra—sleep state
jnana—wakeful, intelligent, awareness
alambanam—support, dependence, help
va—or

39* *yathabhimata*—selected thing, pleasing thing to one's taste
dhyanat—by meditation
va—or

40* *paramanu*—an atom
paramamahattvantah—most distant, most excellent
asya—of this
vasikarah—having mastery over passion, or in one's power

41* *ksina*—dissolving of the *gunas*
vrtteh—modifications
abhijatasya—inborn, noble, polite, worthy
iva—like
maneh—a gem, a flawless crystal
grahitr—knower, taker, perceiver
grahana—at of seizing, catching
grahyesu—to be known
tatstha—becoming stable
tadanjanata—acquiring or taking the shape of the seen or known
samapattih—transformation, assuming the original form
ksinavrtteh—together as one, when fluctuations of the mind are weakened

42* *tatra*—there
sabda—word
artha—purpose
jnana—knowledge, intelligence
vikalpaih—an option, imagination
sankirna—poured together, mixed together
savitarka—becoming totally engrossed
samapattih—transformation

43* *smrti*—memory
   parisuddhau—completely cleansed
   svarupasunya—devoid of one's nature
   iva—as it were
   arthamatranirbhasa—shining alone in its purest form
   nirvitarka—unreflecting, unconsidered, without analysis or logic

44* *etaya*—by this
   eva—also
   savicara—reflection, deliberate
   nirvicara—without reflection, not needing any consideration
   ca—and
   suksmavisayka—subtle object, subtle thing
   vyakhyata—related, explained, commented upon

45* *suksmavisayatvam*—subtle object
   ca—and
   aligna—having no characteristic mark
   paryavasanam—ending

46* *ta*—they
   eva—only
   sabijah—with seed
   samadhih—profound meditation

47* *nirvicara*—nonreflective
   vaisaradye—skillfulness, undisturbed flow
   adhyatma—supreme soul
   prasadah—clearness, brightness, serenity of disposition

48* *rtambhara*—upholding truth, full of intellectual essence
   tatra—therein
   prajna—faculty of insight

49* *sruta*—heard, listened
   anumana—interference
   prajnabhyam—from the wisdom of insights
   anyavisaya—other object
   visesa—peculiar, distinguishing between
   arthatvat—object, purpose, aim

50* *tajjah*—born
samskarah—conceptions, instinct, impressions
anyasamskara—other conceptions, impressions, or formations
pratibandhi—contracting, impeding

51* *tasyapi*—that too
nirodhe—by shutting, closing, restraining, destroying
sarva—all
nirodhat—checking, suppressing
nirbijah—seedless
samadhih—profound meditation

52* *tapah*—heat, devotion, self-discipline
svadhyaya—self-study, understanding self from the outer to the inner body
isvara—God, Lord, or all
pranidhanani—turning in, surrender, bow
kriyayogah—yoga of action

53* *samadhi*—profound meditation
bhavana—for bringing about
arthah—contemplating with meaning and feeling
klesa—afflictions
tanukaranar—for the purpose of thinning, making slender, fine
thah—weakening
ca—and, both

54* *avidya*—spiritual ignorance, lack of knowledge
asmita—ego, pride, I
raja—desire, attachment, passion, pleasure, musical mode
dvesa—hate, dislike, aversion
abhinivesa—love of life, fear of death, clinging to life, leaning to attachment
klesha—affliction, pain, distress, sorrow

55* *avidya*—lack of knowledge, spiritual ignorance
ksetram—a place, a field, fertile soil
uttaresam—that which follows, subsequent
prasupta—asleep, dormant

tanu—thin, lean, delicate
vicchinna—interrupted, hidden
udaranam—fully active

56* *anitya*—not eternal
asuci—impure
duhkha—sorrow, pain
anatmasu—not spiritual, corporeal
nitya—eternal, everlasting, constant
suci—pure
sukha—pleasure, joy
atma—soul
khyatih—opinion, idea, view
avidya—ignorance

57* *drk*—power of vision, cause to see
darsana—power of seeing, looking, displaying, inspecting
saktyoh—ability, capability, strength
ekatmata—same nature, same manner
iva—appearance
asmita—egoism

58* *sukha*—happiness, delight
anusayi—close connection, close attachment
rajah—love affection, musical mode

59* *duhka*—unpleasantness, sorrow, grief
anusayi—close connection, close attachment
dvesah—aversion, hate, dislike, distaste

60* *svarasadhi*—current of love, of life
vidusah—a scholar, wise man, a learned man
api—even, likely
tatha—all the same
arudhah—having ascended, advanced
abhinivesah—intentness of affection, leaning toward, attachment to life

61* *te*—these
   prati—in opposition, against
   prasava—procreation, generation
   heyah—to abandon, desert, relinquish, abstain
   suksmah—subtle, delicate

62* *dhyana*—mediation, reflection, attention
   heyah—rejection, avoided, silenced
   tad—their
   vrttayah—fluctuations, movements, operations

63* *klesa*—affliction, pain, distress, sorrow
   mulah—root, origin
   karma—action, deed
   asayah—reservoir, asylum
   drsta—visible, capable of being seen, perceivable
   adrsta—not capable of being seen, unobservable, fate
   janma—birth, life
   vedanivah—to be known, to be experienced

64* *sati*—being, existing, real, essential, tone
   mule—root
   tat—its
   vipakah—fruit, ripening
   jati—rank, birth, class
   ayuh—span of life
   bhogah—experiencing, enjoying

65* *te*—they
   hlada—pleasant, delighted, rejoiced
   paritapa—pain, anguish, grief
   phalah—fruits
   punya—virtue, asset
   apunya—vices, liability
   hetutvat—being cause by, on account of

66* *parinama*—change, alteration, consequence, result
tapa—heat, torment, pain, sorrow, affliction, distress
samskara—impressions, refinement, conception, instinct
duhkhaih—unhappiness, pain, sorrow, misery
guna—qualities, characteristics
vrtti—fluctuations
virodhat—on account of opposition, obstruction, restraint, contrast
ca—and
dukhham—pain, sorrow
eva—indeed
sarvam—all, whole
vivekinah—the enlightened, man of discrimination

67* *heyam*—to be avoided, to be rejected, to be prevented
duhkham—sorrow, agony
anagatam—not yet come, future, unknown

68* *drastra*—seer, self, *pmrusaa*
drsyayoh—the seen, the known, nature
samyogah—union, association, conjunction, connection, mingling
heyah—to be relinquished, to be avoided
hetuh—cause, ground, reason, purpose

69* *prakasa*—brightness, clearness, splendor
kriya—action, study, investigation
sthiti—steady, firm, steadfast
silam—disposition, virtue, character
bhutam—elements
indriya—the eleven senses, mind, five senses of perception, five organs of action
atmakam—nature or essence of a thing, being composed of
bhoga—enjoyment of pleasure
aparvarga—emancipation, liberation
artham—means, purpose
drsyam—knowable, seen

70* *visesa*—a mark, the art of distinguishing or discriminating
avisesa—uniform, alike, without any difference, unspecified state
lingamatra—indicator, mark, sign, phenomenal, observed

alingani—without a mark, without sign, nonprimary matter or unevolved matter, unknown

gunaparvani—changes in quality

71* *drasta*—seer, *purusa*
drsimatrah—awareness only, consciousness only
suddhah—pure
api—even though
pratyayah—conviction, trust, reliance, faith, cognition, confidence
anupasyah—one who sees, seeing along with, cognizing ideas

72* *tadarthah*—for that purpose, for that sake
eva—alone
drsyaya—of the seen, of the knowable, nature
atma—seer, soul, witness

73* *krtartham*—whose purpose has been fulfilled who has attained an end
prati—against, in opposition to
nastam—destroyed, disappeared, lost sight of
api—although
anastam—not disappeared, not destroyed, not lost
tat—that
anya—to others
sadharanatvat—average, being normal

74* *sva*—one's own, nature, owned
svami—owner, master, lord, seer
saktyoh—strength of prakriti and purusa, power of the two
svarupa—form, one's own
upalabhdhi—to find, obtain, perceive, to see, to recognize
hetuh—cause, reaction, purpose
samyogah—union, conjunction

75* *tasya*—of that
hetuh—cause, ground, purpose
avidya—ignorance, lack of awareness, lack of spiritual knowledge

76* *tad*—it's
abhavat—from nonexistence, from absence, from nonentity

samyogah—union, association, conjunction
abhavah—absence, disappearance
hanmam—an act of leaving, stopping, removing, remedying
tad—that
drseh—if the knower, seer
kaivalyam—absolute freedom, emancipation, absorption in the supreme soul

77* *viveka*—discrimination, judgment, true knowledge
khyatih—the faculty of discriminating objects by an appropriate designation
aviplava—undisturbed, unbroken, unfailing
hanopayah—the means of removal, the means for dispersion

78* *tasya*—it's
saptadha—sevenfold, of seven stages
prantabhumih—territory, province, resting place
prajna—perfect knowledge, supreme knowledge, awareness

79* *yoga*—to join, to yoke
anga—components, aspects
anusthanat—by devoted practice
asuddhih—impurities
ksaye—diminished, destroyed
jnana—knowledge, wisdom
diptih—shines forth, radiates
avivekakhyateh—the essence of knowledge, the glory of knowledge

80* *yama*—self-restraint
niyama—rules, orders, observances
asana—shapes, postures, seat
pranayama—breath regulation, retention of breath
pratyahara—retreat, withdrawal of the senses
dharana—the act of concentration
dhyana—meditation, contemplation, reflection
samadhayah—putting together, collection, profound meditation
astau—eight
angani—limb

81* *ahimsa*—harmlessness, nonviolence, not to strike or hit
satya—truth, real, genuine, honest, virtuous
asteya—nonstealing
brahmacarya—chastity, moderation
aparigrahah—without possessions
yamah—self-restraint

82* *jati*—class of birth, lineage
desa—place, spot, country
kala—time
samaya—condition or circumstance
anavacchinnah—not limited, not bound
sarvabhaumah—relating to or consisting of the whole world
mahavratam—mighty vow, great obligation

83* *sauca*—cleanliness, purity
santosa—contentment
tapah—religious fervor, a burning desire
svadhyaya—self-study
isvara pranidhanani—surrender to God, concentration on God
niyama—established observance

84* *vitarka*—questionable or dubious matter, doubt, uncertainty
badhane—pain, suffering, grief
pratipaksa—the opposite side, to the contrary
bhavanam—affecting, creating, promoting

85* *vitarkah*—dubious knowledge
himsa—of violence, injuries
adayah—and so forth
krta—done
karita—caused to be done, induced, aroused
anumoditah—permitted to be
lobha—desire, greed
krodha—anger
moha—delusion, infatuation
purvakah—preceded by, caused by
mrdu—mild, slight
madhya—moderate, medium

adhimatrah—intense, sharp
duhkha—pain, sorrow
ajnana—ignorance
ananta—endless, infinite
phalah—fruit, result
iti—thus
pratipaksa—contrary thoughts
bhavanam—feeling, resting place

86* *ahimsa*—nonviolence
pratisthayam—standing firmly, firmly established
tat—his
sannidhau—presence, vicinity
vaira—animosity, hostility
tyagah—forsaken, abandoning, deserting

87* *satya*—truth, sincerity, genuineness, honestly
pratisthayam—standing firmly, firmly established
kriya—action
phalah—results
asrayattva—foundation

88* *asteya*—nonstealing, nonmisappropriation, desirelessness
pratisthayam—standing firmly, firmly established
sarva—all
ratna—gems, precious things
upasthanam—approaching, coming up

89* *brahmacarya*—continence, chastity
pratisthayam—well established
virya—energy, vigor, potency, valor
labhah—gained, obtained

90* *aparigraha*—without possessions, without belongings, nonacceptance of gifts
sthairye—by becoming steady, stable
janma—birth
kathamta—how, in what way, in what manner
sambodha—knowledge, illusion

91* *saucat*—by cleanliness, by purity
sva—self
anga—limbs, body
jugupsa—censure, dislike, aversion, being on one's guard
paraih—with others
asamsargah—noncontact, nonintercourse

92* *sattvasuddhi*—purity in the essence of consciousness
sau—benevolent, pleasing, cheerful
manasya—mind
ekagra—concentration, fixity
indriya—senses of perception and organs of action
jaya—controlled, conquered
atma—self, soul
darsana—knowledge, vision
yogyatvani—fitness to see
ca—and also

93* *santosat*—contentment
anuttamah—unexcelled, unsurpassed, supreme, excellent
sukha—delight, happiness
labhah—gain

94* *kaya*—body
indriya—senses
siddhih—attainment, power
asuddhi—impurities
ksayat—destruction
tapasah—ascetic devotion, a burning desire to reach perfection, that which burns away impurities, self-discipline

95* *svadhyayat*—by study that leads to self-knowledge, self-study, reading scriptures
istadevata—the desired deity
samprayoga—union, communion, coming in contact with the divine

96* *samadhi*—absorption, profound meditation, super consciousness
siddhih—accomplishment, success
Isvara—God
pranidhanat—by surrender, by resignation, by application

⁹⁷* *sthira*—firm, fixed, steady
sukham—happiness, delight
asanam—postures, poses

⁹⁸* *prayatna*—persevering effort, continued exertion
saithilya—laxity, relaxation
ananta—endless, boundless, eternal, infinite
samapattibhyam—assuming original form, completion, conclusion

⁹⁹* *tatah*—from that, then
dvandvah—dualities, opposites
anabhighatah—cessation of disturbances

¹⁰⁰* *tasmin*—on this
sati—being accomplished
svasa—in breath, inhalation
prasvasayoh—outward breath, exhalation
gatti—movement, motion, path
vicchedah—cessation, stoppage, interruption
pranayamah—extension, expansion, regulation of breath

¹⁰¹* *bahya*—external
abhyantara—internal
stambha—restrain, suspension, a pause
vrittih—movement
desa—place
kala—time, duration
samkhyabhih—number, precision, reflection, deliberation
paridrstah—regulated, measured
dirgha—long in place and time, expansion, high
suksmah—subtle, soft, fine, exquisite

¹⁰²* *bahya*—external
abhyantara—internal
visaya—region, an object, reference, aim
aksepi—passing over, gaining over, overcoming
caturthah—the fourth

[103*] *tataḥ*—from that, then
kṣiyate—destroyed, dissolved
prakāśa—light
āvaraṇam—covering

[104*] *dhāraṇāsu*—for concentration
ca—and
yogyatā—fitness, suitability, propriety, ability, capability, appropriateness
manasaḥ—of mind

[105*] *sva*—their own
viṣaya—objects
asamprayoge—not coming in contact with
cittasya—of the thinking faculty, of the mind faculty
svarūpa—own form, natural form
anukāraḥ—imitating, following
iva—as if, as it were
indriyāṇām—senses
pratyāhāraḥ—to draw toward the opposite, drawing back, retreating, restraining, withholding

[106*] *tataḥ*—then, from that
parama—the highest
vaśyatā—subdued, controlled, governed
indriyāṇām—of the senses

Made in the USA
Coppell, TX
30 January 2024